Contingent Liability Management

A Study on India

Tarun Das • Anil Bisen • M. R. Nair • Raj Kumar

Commonwealth Secretariat

Commonwealth Secretariat
Marlborough House
Pall Mall, London SW1Y 5HX
United Kingdom

Designed by KC Gan designs
Cover illustration by Diane Allard
Printed by Hobbs the Printers, Southampton

Published by the Commonwealth Secretariat
ISBN: 0-85092-709-0

Copies of this publication may be obtained from:
The Publications Manager
Information and Public Affairs Division
Commonwealth Secretariat
Pall Mall, London SW1Y 5HX
United Kingdom

Tel: +44 (0)20 7747 6342
Fax: +44 (0)20 7839 9081
Email: r.jones-parry@commonwealth.int
Websites: http://www.thecommonwealth.org

Contents

Acknowledgements

This report has been put together by a team comprising Dr Tarun Das, Economic Adviser; Mr Anil Bisen, Director, from the Ministry of Finance; Mr M. R. Nair, Adviser, from the Reserve Bank of India; and Dr Raj Kumar, Special Economic Adviser, from the Commonwealth Secretariat, London. The views contained in the report are the personal views of the members and not necessarily those of the institutions they represent.

The team wishes to place on record its appreciation for the contributions of Sarvashri B. N. Anatha Swamy, Somnath Chatterjee, Sitikantha Pattanaik, Muneesh Kapur and A. Karunagaran of the Reserve Bank of India; Mr Arindam Roy and Mr Krishan Kumar of the Ministry of Finance, Government of India; and Mr Dev Useree of the Commonwealth Secretariat.

The team is grateful to Ms Catherine Gondwe of the Commonwealth Secretariat for her services in putting the various contributions into an integrated document.

The team appreciates the comments received during a presentation in Washington of the draft report in November 2000 and wishes to acknowledge in particular the input provided by Hana Polackova Brixi, Sergei Shatalov, Fred Jensen, A. Mody and Malvina Pollock. The report has benefited from funds from the Institutional Development Facility of the World Bank for India, and acknowledgement must be made to the Commonwealth Fund for Technical Co-operation, the operational arm of the Commonwealth Secretariat.

Foreword

The sharp increase in the contingent liabilities of many developing countries in recent years and its possible implications has prompted a rethink in the way governments quantify their fiscal burdens. The increase in contingent liabilities is primarily attributed to the transformation of the role of the state from a supplier of certain services to a facilitator, where the state extends a guarantee to the private sector for providing such services. Contingent liabilities of the government have also increased due to liberalization of the capital account by many countries as well as the move towards greater integration of international financial markets.

Recognizing the significant rise in the contingent liabilities-both external and implicit- of many countries and concerns on potential risks this may entail, the Commonwealth Secretariat has been placing greater emphasis on the need for monitoring such exposures. As part of its programme of advisory services on debt and development resource management, the Debt Management Services Department of the Special Advisory Services Division (DMS-SASD)* has been encouraging governments in explicitly taking into account their contingent liabilities while gauging the risks associated with countries' debt portfolios.

The publication of this report on contingent liability management is topical and timely indeed. While highlighting the basic conceptual issues on the subject matter it looks at some of the issues related to the identification, monitoring and valuation of external sector contingent liabilities of India. It also attempts to define a framework that can be used for measuring these liabilities.

The report is being disseminated to a wider audience with the objective of sharing India's experience so far in external sector contingent liability management and also to influence both thought and action, especially at a time when there is growing need for countries to assess their overall financial risks and vulnerabilities emerging from changes in the external economic environment. We hope that policy makers in central banks and ministries of finance will find this report useful. We would welcome any comments on this publication.

Richard Gold
Director
Special Advisory Services Division
Commonwealth Secretariat

---

*   The Debt Management Programme was previously housed in the Economic and Legal Advisory Services Division (ELASD)

1. Introduction

Background

The significance of monitoring contingent liabilities for macro-economic and financial stability has been clearly recognised both in academic and policy circles. The recent East Asian crisis has only re-emphasised how important it is for governments to monitor and manage their contingent liabilities. One of the features of the East Asian crisis was the triggering of a range of contingent liabilities, which put a strain on the fiscal position of the governments concerned.

These contingent liabilities, mainly in the form of government guarantees, have been used to promote both foreign and local investment in projects. However, the crisis confirmed the need for better assessment of the potential risks that could emerge from contingent liabilities under various scenarios, and the need to develop more effective systems to monitor and manage them. Indeed, contingent liabilities can be a major factor in the build-up of public debt.

The sharp increase in the contingent liabilities of many countries in recent years and the change in the nature of the financial burden of the fiscal authorities has been primarily attributed to the transformation of the role of the state from a supplier of certain services (for instance, infrastructure) to a facilitator, where the state extends a guarantee to the private sector for providing such services. Other contributory factors have been the liberalisation of the capital account and the integration of international financial markets. While globalisation and greater access to foreign capital facilitated a more efficient mobilisation of resources, the vicissitudes of private capital flows, as evidenced by the East Asian crisis, exacerbated the vulnerability of emerging market economies to sudden shifts in market sentiment, which almost inevitably, induced a sharp reversal of flows.

The subsequent bailing out of insolvent banks and corporates reflects the hidden contingent liabilities of these governments. Furthermore, the redeeming of such contingent liabilities, mostly at short notice, could considerably strain government finances.

Another factor responsible for the increase in fiscal risks is the cash-based budgetary accounting framework adopted by many economies, which records the financial impact of contingent liabilities, not on an accrual basis but when expenditure actually takes place. Given the bias in cash-based budgetary systems towards actual transactions that occur, liabilities that were of a contingent nature were either ignored or took an "off-budget" character. Consequently, there was limited monitoring of such contingent liabilities and, in some instances, these liabilities multiplied without adequate provision in the budget. In a sense, a perverse incentive (fiscal opportunism) can create the potential for governments to incur such liabilities that neither involve immediate financing, nor are reflected in conventional measures of deficit that could be closely monitored.

A World Bank report on the Czech Republic by Polackova et al (1999) indicated that while the conventional fiscal deficit of the Czech government was in general, placed below 2 per cent of GDP during the second half of the 1990s, the hidden deficit which reflected net spending on programmes of a fiscal nature by special off-budget institutions and implicit subsidies extended through state guarantees, ranged between 1 and 3 per cent of GDP. To the extent that contingent liabilities may involve severe future cash outflows (particularly in the case of default by private entities) these may have unfortunate consequences for the fiscus in particular, and the economy in general.

In the United States of America too, the sharp increase in contingent liabilities during the 1970s as a result of government guarantee programmes, including loans to corporations, mortgage and deposit insurance, and trade and exchange rate guarantees, did not show up explicitly in the budget, but their impact was subsequently felt when the federal deposit insurance had to make up for the losses of the savings and loans industry in the late 1980s. The World Bank's Global Development Finance (1999) indicated that nearly half the increase in direct sovereign liabilities over the past decade may be attributable to the honoring of contingent and implicit government liabilities, some of which related to external obligations.

In India the subject of the more effective monitoring of contingent liabilities, especially those relating to the external sector, has been under consideration for some time. The Report of the Technical Group on External Debt (1998) also emphasised, inter alia, the need for monitoring external contingent liabilities in India. The group recommended that appropriate institutional arrangements might be put in place to capture such information on an ongoing basis.

The scope and structure of the report

The subject of contingent liability encompasses both the external and domestic sectors. From the budgetary perspective, contingent liabilities have to take both these sectors into account. The focus of the report, however, is mostly on external sector contingent liabilities that involve possible financial transactions with non-residents. At times, however, the split between external and domestic sector contingent liabilities may not be clear-cut.

External sector contingent liabilities, once triggered, could increase the level of external public debt and lead to balance of payment consequences. The consideration of external sector contingent liabilities together with external debt in an integrated way, could bring out external debt management and operations issues more forcefully.

A separate study on guarantees provided by state governments in India has already been conducted, which highlights some of the issues relevant to domestic sector, contingent liabilities. (See Report of the Technical Committee on State Government Guarantees, Reserve Bank of India, February 1999).

This report does not attempt to value the total contingent liabilities of India and the underlying risks, which will be a subsequent activity once the issues of identifying contingent liabilities and their valuation has been decided. However, wherever feasible, areas of exposure to external contingent liabilities have been considered.

Against this backdrop, this report focuses on some of the issues which are relevant to the identification, monitoring and valuation of external sector contingent liabilities. Chapter 2 provides a definition of contingent liabilities, clarifies a number of conceptual issues regarding their possible impact on the nation's indebtedness and outlines alternative techniques for their evaluation. Chapter 3 provides an account of country experiences in dealing with contingent liabilities. Chapter 4 deals with government of India guarantees on external debt and how the government policy towards guarantees has evolved over time. Chapter 5 focuses on contingent liabilities relating to infrastructure investment. Chapter 6 analyses the contingent liabilities of the banking, financial institutions and corporate sectors in India. The last chapter contains conclusions and a summary of the recommendations.

2. Definitional and Conceptual Issues

The fiscal risk matrix

Contingent liabilities may be defined as contractual financial arrangements that give rise to conditional requirements, either to make payments or to provide objects of value (System of National Accounts, 1993). For the financial transaction to take place, one or more conditions must be fulfilled. A key characteristic that makes such liabilities different from normal financial transactions is that they are uncertain. Contingent liabilities are not easy to quantify and standards to measure them are evolving. Furthermore, in cash-based systems of accounts they are not always fully covered, as no transactions are associated with the creation of these obligations.

It is perhaps expedient to begin with the conventional framework for analysing contingent liabilities of the government in the form of a fiscal risk matrix. Liabilities may be classified as "direct", i.e. those that would arise in any event and are therefore certain and predictable, or contingent, i.e. those that may or may not be incurred, depending on the occurrence of a particular event. For instance, the timing and amount of the contractual obligation is fixed on the date of issue of a government loan (i.e. a direct liability), whereas the obligation in the case of a government guarantee (i.e. a contingent liability) would depend on the time and magnitude of default by the borrower. In general, contingent liabilities refer to obligations to provide for a possible default by a borrower on the principal and/or interest of the loan.

Contingent liabilities may be funded, i.e. matched by a reserve or charge against profits equal to the actuarial (present discounted) value of expected "payouts", or unfunded. Both direct and contingent liabilities may, in turn, be classified as "explicit" i.e. those that are defined by law or contract, or "implicit" i.e. those that are incurred on "moral" grounds or as a result of public and interest group pressures. Direct contingent liabilities include deposit insurance as well as official guarantees for private/public sector borrowings, wherein the maximum possible liability on the guarantor is clearly defined ex ante. Implicit contingent liabilities, on the other hand, are not officially recognised until the "default" occurs and therefore, the amount of expenditure that would ultimately be required is uncertain. Government support (beyond deposit insurance) for failed financial institutions, particularly when such failure is systemic, is generally the most serious form of contingent implicit liability.

External sector contingent liabilities

The fiscal risk framework shown in Box 2.1 could be adapted to cover external-sector related contingent liabilities. Box 2.2 provides examples of the varies types of contingent liabilities related to the external sector that countries may wish to monitor.

Box 2.1: The fiscal risk matrix

Liabilities	Direct	Contingent
Explicit	Foreign or domestic sovereign borrowing	Government guarantees for non-sovereign borrowing, trade and exchange rate guarantees issued by the government, deposit insurance, income from private pension funds, flood insurance
Implicit	Social security schemes, future public pensions and future health care financing if not required by law	Banking failure (support beyond deposit insurance), bailouts following a reversal in private capital flows

Resident and non-resident

In analysing a country's external contingent liabilities, there is a need to distinguish between contingent external transactions such as guarantees effected (a) between residents and (b) between a resident and a non-resident. In the former case, contingent external liabilities would "cancel out" at the national level to the extent that the "underlying transaction" (e.g. an external loan) is already recorded under the country's direct external liability. For instance, guarantees given by commercial banks on the external commercial borrowings (ECBs) of (domestic) corporates are contingent liabilities of the commercial banks, but such liabilities do not increase the direct external liabilities of the country since ECBs already form a part.

So, a default by the borrower is "made good" by the guarantor and this does not entail any additional liability for the country as a whole. In the latter case, if the underlying transaction is not part of the resident country's direct external liability (for example, if a non-resident bank has extended a loan to another non-resident in a different country against a guarantee provided by a resident bank) then the contingent liability would be over and above what is reported under the total liabilities of the resident country. With the further liberalisation of the capital account, the magnitude of such liabilities is likely to increase, and if not managed effectively, has the potential to create systemic risks.

Derivative transactions

In the same vein, with respect to derivative transactions, it needs to be recognised that, to the extent that the underlying transaction has already been captured under the debt or non-debt liabilities of the country, for example, in the case of Financial Institutional Investor (FII) inflows, the derivative transaction would not have any impact on the volume of total direct external liabilities, provided that the market valuation principle in respect of derivatives has been identified and captured.

Box 2.2: Examples of external sector contingent liabilities

Liabilities of Fiscal Activities	Direct (Obligations in any event)	Contingent (Obligations if a particular event occurs)
Explicit Government liability as recognised by law, contract or insurance policy	Foreign sovereign borrowings (loans contracted and securities issued by central government, and held by non-residents) Commitments to multilateral agencies e.g. IBRD, Asian Development Bank	State guarantees for non-sovereign borrowing from non-residents Exchange rate and trade related guarantees (e.g. exchange rate guarantees, forward arrangements, letters of credit) Indemnities and guarantees relating to external-sector related infrastructure project or recently privatised enterprises External guarantees provided by nationalised banks, developmental financial institutions, EXIM Bank
Implicit A "moral obligation of government that reflects systematic risk considerations and public expectations"	Future recurrent costs of public investment projects implemented under BOT, BOO schemes involving the participation of foreign investors	Default of an institutional government and public or private entity on external non-guaranteed debt and other external liabilities Clearing the liabilities of privatised entities with significant foreign participation Failure of strategically important private sector projects leading to their return to the public sector. Bank failure (beyond state institutions) where deposits of non-residents are also affected Investment failure of a state-run investment fund with participation by foreigners Default of the central bank on its obligations (foreign exchange contracts) Environmental damage affecting offshore areas, where foreign claims are involved.

On the other hand, if a derivative contract is effected by a foreign branch of a resident bank with another non-resident whose claims are on third parties (and hence not recorded as part of the resident country's liabilities) then it would amount to a contingent liability, since the foreign branch would take on the obligation to sell foreign exchange in the forward market. Thus, obtaining information on these types of exposures, particularly proprietary trading activities of foreign branches is essential for monitoring the risk exposure of a branch that may jeopardise the capital base of the parent bank; to that extent such exposure could be classified as a contingent liability of the parent.

Exchange valuation

With regard to the treatment of exchange valuation losses relating to direct external liabilities that may be thought of as a contingent liability, it needs to be recognised that these losses entail only a domestic currency obligation and, given the extant system of periodically valuing the external debt of the country at prevalent exchange rates, do not result in an incremental direct obligation in terms of foreign currency. So even though certain transactions may not be strictly classified as contingent liabilities, it is necessary to monitor them as they could have adverse implications for financial stability.

Contingent liabilities in the emerging economy context

The World Bank has identified three areas that can give rise to particularly large contingent liabilities (Sound Practices in Sovereign Debt Management, World Bank, March 2000). These are as follows:

- Many governments are in the process of privatising their infrastructure and are seeking private sector participants in new infrastructure development. These policy goals have frequently been accompanied by requests from the private sector for guarantees or, in the case of privatisation, for the government to assume the debts of the state-owned enterprise prior to its sale. (This is considered in the next section and also in greater depth in Chapter 5, given its growing importance to India.)

- The nature of the financial sector regulatory and supervisory framework in emerging markets can lead to excessive risk-taking by private sector financial intermediaries, especially as new opportunities arise with financial sector deregulation and capital account liberalisation. The added systemic risk can substantially increase a government's implicit contingent obligations.

- Macro-economic policy imbalances, often in conjunction with inefficient regulatory policies, have often led to overvalued real exchange rates and governments have sometimes incurred substantial losses in endeavouring to defend a fixed exchange rate anchor.

The Financial Stability Forum has also considered these areas and has given recommendations on government risk management. (See Box 2.3)

Box 2.3: The financial stability forum: The report of the working group on capital flow aspects relating to contingent liabilities and government risk management (selected recommendations)

The public sector

Too often the goal of public debt management has been viewed narrowly as how to borrow at the lowest interest rates. Recent crises have made it clear that a government needs a more prudent, integrated debt and asset management strategy. The strategy should strike a balance between the expected costs and risks, including the liquidity risk. It should cover domestic and foreign currency assets and liabilities, and it should cover all parts of the public sector, even if only to make clear which parts of the public sector carry a guarantee from the central government. Although country circumstances vary, there are common issues that influence what might be both a prudent and practical course for a country.

The group formulated a checklist of issues relating to sovereign risk management that it believes national authorities should consider:

A government should develop a strategy for public sector risk and liquidity management. It should cover all the obligations and claims of the public sector, including contingent obligations and claims, in both domestic and foreign currencies.

The government's liquidity strategy should take into account the extent to which pressure could be placed on its liquidity, in domestic and foreign currencies, by interactions with other sectors of the economy including among many other things, the withdrawal of resident or non-resident domestic or foreign currency deposits from the domestic banking system.

The government should monitor and manage the contingent liabilities it incurs via explicit deposit protection schemes and any other investor protection schemes, and should aim to avoid creating an expectation that it will guarantee the financial sector's obligations beyond any such explicit schemes.

Where the public sector's overall balance sheet structure leaves it exposed to a material risk of liquidity crisis, the authorities should identify and implement measures to reduce those risks.

Where the private sector is found to have become unusually vulnerable to a liquidity crisis or to shocks which could jeopardise its solvency (e.g. via a large exchange rate exposure), the public authorities should consider measures both directly to reduce those risks and to avoid their being exacerbated by public sector liquidity management problems.

If a government contemplates issuing or investing in complex financial instruments, it should obtain expert advice, taking care to understand the incentives of the advisers, in particular whether they will gain from a particular deal. It should ensure that it understands, and has obtained advice on, the sensitivity of the value of the liability or investment to different world states. It should also assess the counter-party risk involved; and reflect other particular features of the liabilities or investments in its stress-testing exercises.

To support such a sovereign asset and liability management strategy, national authorities should have at their disposal an accounting of official assets and liabilities. This should include not only the items on their balance sheets, but contingent liabilities and other off-balance sheet items, as well. It should include not only financial contracts, but also the public sector's other sources of income and obligations. Moreover, the authorities should have a systematic picture of the maturity profile (or amortisation schedule) and other characteristics of the official sector's debt.

Source: Report of the Working Group on Capital Flows, Financial Stability Forum, 5 April 2000

Public contingent liabilities in private infrastructure projects

The growing trend of infrastructure privatisation and other forms of private sector participation such as Build Operate Transfer (BOT) and variants, have accelerated infrastructure developments and operations, and reduced direct government budgetary expenditure. Given that such investments are large and their costs can only be recovered over a long period of time, there are inherent risks, which have resulted in a sharing of the risks between private investors and the government.

Although investors assume the commercial risks of the project (e.g. construction and operations) they are not willing to bear those sovereign risks against which they cannot hedge. In many cases, and India is no exception, governments are asked to bear residual risks associated with these projects, which can amount to substantial contingent liabilities. Host governments provide a range of guarantees depending on the characteristics of the project as well as the nature of country risks. Some typical examples of risks assumed by governments are summarised below:

Demand risk

This is usually a commitment by the host government to ensure that the private investor receives a minimum level of revenue when demand is lower than expected. For example, minimum traffic levels for roads and bridges are specified, and the government is required to reimburse tariffs on a pre-determined formula if the traffic falls below this level (e.g. The El Cortijo-El Vino toll project in Columbia and the M5 motorway in Hungary). Another example is where governments, through their utility enterprises, have agreed to pay private power producers a fixed amount each year that is independent of the actual level of power subsequently demanded by them.

Payment risk

This usually takes the form of the government guaranteeing the payments of the utility it owns if it were unable to meet its liabilities to the investor, especially for power projects (e.g. the Tanzania Songo Songo Power project).

Exchange and interest rate risk

There have been cases of the government bearing full or partial exchange and interest rates risks on foreign loans, bonds and credits that financed the project. For example, the Spanish government spent about $2.7 billion as a result of such guarantees provided to toll road concessions. The Pakistan government ensured foreign exchange convertibility for its Lal Pir project. The Malaysian government provided interest rate and exchange rate guarantees relating to the North-South Highway project. Such guarantees will become less of a concern as currency and interest swap and forward markets develop.

Political and regulatory risk

There are risks that are tied to actions taken, or influenced by the government's political considerations. For example, the Malaysian government prevented a road toll rise, reducing the profitability of the contractor, which resulted in a renegotiation of terms and conditions and a higher financial burden on the government.

Implied risk-bearing

Not all risks are explicit in contracts or laws. The East Asian crisis has showed many examples in Malaysia and Thailand where the government, through its debt agencies, agreed to bear the credit risk taken on banks in respect of privatisation projects. Box 2.4 shows how a sudden devaluation of a currency and significant current account deficits of the kind experienced in East Asia in 1997 can adversely affect infrastructure projects financed by BOO-BOT schemes, and create substantial contingent liabilities for the government.

Box 2.4: Build Own Transfer (BOT) and Build Own Operate (BOO) schemes

Recent public risk experience

- It is often assumed that the use of financing techniques such as Build Own Transfer (BOT) and Build Own Operate (BOO) in Asian private infrastructure programmes, relieves the host country from the liabilities associated with financing, building and operating infrastructure projects. This is a misconception. The reality is that many of the risks of the project remain with the host government under the support contracts they enter into.

- A typical BOT or BOO structure in Asia would involve a local company, primarily owned by foreign investors, entering into a support contract with the host government under which the company agrees to finance, build, own and operate an infrastructure project, such as a power station or a toll road, for a specified concessionary period.

- The host government in return agrees in the support contract to pay or guarantee tariffs to the local company sufficient to repay the capital costs of the project. The tariffs are set to provide a reasonable rate of return to the investors and to service the debt borrowed to build the project.

- The government gets the benefit of a much needed infrastructure project without having to borrow or spend its own precious foreign currency reserves to build it. This financing technique, together with the enormous need for infrastructure in the region and the voracious appetite of private capital for new investment opportunities in Asia, has created the financing phenomenon of the decade. Estimates vary, but the total value of private infrastructure investment through BOT or BOO schemes in Asia in 1996 alone, is thought to be in the region of $50 billion (£29.90 billion).

- Three features of the government support contracts for these projects, combined with current account deficits of crisis proportion, could transform the private infrastructure development programmes of some Asian countries into a serious sovereign debt problem.

Firstly, the support contracts between the host government and the project company typically provide that the tariff will either be paid in hard currency (usually US dollars) or that the government will guarantee the dollar equivalent amount of local currency payments. Foreign exchange risks are thus allocated to the host government.

Secondly, the support contract will typically provide for a termination payment by the host government in the event that it fails to perform any of its obligations, including the obligation to assure the availability of foreign currency. The termination payments are required by the project company's lenders, who want to ensure that sufficient money is available in a lump sum on government default to repay the debt they advance to finance the project. The termination payments are therefore at least sufficient to repay the project company's outstanding debt.

Thirdly, gearing can be as high as 80:20. High levels of gearing are driven by the economics of these projects. As debt is generally a cheaper form of investment capital than equity, and because these projects are capital-intensive, high levels of debt financing are used to satisfy the competing requirements of governments (low tariffs) and investors (high returns). For collateral, project lenders will charge all the assets of the project company, and take a security assignment of the government support contract.

The result of all this is that governments commit themselves to billions of dollars' worth of contractual obligations, all due in a lump sum, to protect investors and lenders against foreign exchange risk. This is how a project banker's nightmare starts. Debt service payments under project loan agreements are not paid because there is not enough foreign currency available from the host government. A default ensues, and project lenders enforce their security assignment of the government support contract and step into the shoes of the project.

Governments then owe large sums of money to international banks; export credit agencies and multilateral institutions for infrastructure development (which is precisely what the BOT and BOO model was supposed to avoid). The lack of foreign currency that led to the default in the first place means that the government will not be able to make the termination payment.

■ Project lenders could attempt to enforce the termination payment obligation against the host government. But the problem of enforcing termination payment under government support contracts may be more problematic for international lenders than true sovereign debt restructuring. Termination payments under government support contracts are not structured as debt. None of the customary sovereign lending covenants, such as negative pledges and the pari passu clause are included in the contract. The lenders will be uncertain as to the priority their termination payment claims will have *vis-à-vis* true sovereign borrowings.

■ Moreover, inter-credit arrangements in these projects are complex, often involving export credit agencies, multilateral institutions and commercial funders all lending to the same project. These lenders have historically approached sovereign debt restructuring differently and could reasonably be expected to approach termination workouts in a similarly diverse fashion. Achieving the necessary level of consensus among the project lenders to approve a restructuring plan may prove difficult.

(Extract from *The Financial Times*, December 1997)

Independent Power Projects (IPP) and government guarantees

This section is largely drawn from a Public Information Document relating to the Tanzania Songo Songo Gas to Electricity project.

The rationale for the guarantee of utilities

The IPP business is new and in many cases is moving ahead in countries with high country risk profiles, specifically in the power sector which has exhibited poor, past performance. Many developing countries are implementing sector reforms to correct these problems, often with support from the World Bank (e.g. Guatemala, Jamaica, Pakistan, Philippines), including the rehabilitation of existing assets, corporation programmes, regulatory changes and the privatisation of state-owned entities.

Experience shows that the transition period from a state-dominated power sector to one more oriented towards private sector participation can take several years to complete. In the meantime, new capacity needs are often critical to the sustainability of economic growth spurred on by macro-economic reform programmes. Private investors, while encouraged by power sector reforms (regulatory, legal, etc.), nevertheless face an untested environment, and therefore are not willing to assume the risk that state-owned entities will not meet their contractual obligations to the privately-owned IPP. The most significant risk is the payment risk, followed perhaps by transfer risk as IPPs generally do not generate foreign currency, and yet require substantial amounts of foreign exchange financing for imported equipment.

Given this context, it may be appropriate for governments to provide limited guarantees to the project which generally take the form of performance guarantees of state-owned entities, particularly payment guarantees. This reflects the fact that tariff levels and structures are generally controlled by the government. It is also due to the fact that power projects are often at the mercy of a single customer which is almost always a public sector entity, often with a weak balance sheet due to a history of electricity payment arrears or mismanagement. In other words, the government and not the private investors have control over these risks and so are in a better position to assume them.

Even if the utility is corporatised and is operating in a commercial manner, it may lack a sufficient track record of autonomous operation, and still faces these regulatory risks which impact on their ability to pay the IPP investor. In return for these limited guarantees, the government benefits from a significant shift in the construction and operating risks from the public to the private sector. Private investors also assume pre-construction development risks which even in public sector projects are substantial in terms of the time and money spent on developing a power project. Private investors, in addition to feasibility studies and the technical preparation of the project, also have to contend with (and pay for) negotiating various contracts for the sale of electricity and the supply of fuel, among other things. These are costs that the investors bear if the project does not move ahead, which happens fairly frequently.

Recent international experience

Box 2.5 presents some recent independent power projects (IPPs) which have involved government guarantees of certain obligations of the purchasing utilities and other state-owned entities.

Box 2.5: The international experience of Independent Power Projects (IPPs)

Sl.No.	Country	Project/Sponsor	Year	Government Guarantee
1.	Philippines	Pagbilao	1993	payment for electricity fuel supply convertibility
2.	Philippines	Subic Bay	1994	payment for electricity fuel supply convertibility
3.	Jamaica	Rockfort	1994	payment for electricity
4.	Pakistan	Hub	1992	payment for electricity guarantee of fuel supplier's performance.
5.	Guatemala	Puerto Quetzal	1993	payment for electricity
6.	Belize	Macal River Hydro		payment for electricity

7.	India	GKV Industries	1994	payment for electricity from Andhra Pradesh State Electricity Board
8.	India	ST-CMS Electric	1994	payment for electricity from Tamil Nadu Electricity Board
9.	Nepal	Himal Power	1994	payment for electricity

The World Bank is supporting the projects in Pakistan and Jamaica, and the International Finance Corporation (IFC) is supporting the remaining projects. There are examples of projects that have gone ahead without government guarantees, but these should be seen in context. Two examples are the Pangue project in Chile and the YTL project in Malaysia.

In Chile, the power sector has been gradually privatised over the last 15 years, following the passage of an electricity law which provides the framework for private sector participation. This framework is well tested and investors are generally comfortable with it after 15 years of experience. Still, Pangue was the first major private investment undertaken in Chile since privatisation, and even then it involved the IFC taking an important role. Several other projects have been completed since the passage of the law, but these drew on outstanding World Bank and Inter-American Development Bank loans.

In Malaysia the national utility, Tenaga Nasional Berhad (TNB), which is purchasing the power is a state-owned company, but it is a financially strong company run as a commercial entity, which sold 25 per cent of its shares to private investors in Malaysia. The YTL project was, in fact, financed by domestic investors and involved no foreign sources, a scenario not often faced by private sponsors of IPPs. Iso, Standard and Poor then rated Malaysia's sovereign credit A, thus giving investors (domestic or foreign) a significant amount of comfort in the viability of their investment in that country. (Since then, there has been a lowering of this rating following the East Asian crisis).

Questions which governments can pose with respect to IPPs

- Are the risks being borne by the private investors commensurate with the desired rate of return?

- How are the sovereign risks being covered under the project, and are the proposed arrangements reasonable?

- How to mitigate through contractual arrangement risks associated with investment cost over-runs, delays in project commissioning and poor performance by the private investors?

A framework for monitoring contingent liabilities

There can be several approaches to developing a framework for the monitoring and management of contingent liabilities. It will be highly dependent on the range of contingent liabilities and the legal and institutional arrangements in a country. Emerging market economies have areas of special monitoring with respect to vulnerabilities introduced in the process of economic and financial liberalisation.

There are three approaches which could be defined as follows, although it is recognised that they are inter-related.

1. **The integrated budget approach**

    This approach comes from the Code of Good Practices on Fiscal Transparency developed by the IMF. The Code maintains that the budget should disclose the main central government contingent liabilities, provide a brief indication of their nature and indicate the potential beneficiaries. The Code suggests that the best practice would involve providing an estimate of the expected cost of each contingent liability whenever possible and the basis for estimating expected costs.

    As discussed in the next chapter, the integrated budget approach is the most common in developed economies such as the United States, United Kingdom, Canada, Australia and New Zealand.

2. **The asset-liability framework**

    A government asset-liability (A-L) management framework is a valuable conceptual framework for considering, among other matters, the management of fiscal risks and risk-sharing arrangements with the private sector. Included in this framework are both financial and contingent liabilities and associated risks. The A-L framework is basically a government balance sheet. In this model, contingent liabilities are priced on a risk-adjusted basis.

    This framework is applicable to financial intermediaries managing both a lending book and a funding portfolio. However, as a consequence of the varied and complex nature of contingent liabilities of the government, and the fact that these are dispersed across various sectors, these liabilities cannot be easily analysed within an asset-liability framework based on a government balance sheet. In any case, even though "net worth" calculations are not normally shown by governments, the A-L framework with contingent liabilities as an integral component of the liabilities in the government balance sheet remains an important mechanism for managing risk.

    Such a framework, however, has to recognise that the types of risk and the way the government manages risks differs from those of the private sector. First of all, there are risks which the government bears for which markets do not exist (e.g. the failure of a bank). Secondly, the government has a greater ability than the private sector to hold reserves and/or raise taxes and other revenue should there be a big disaster (e.g. the Kobe earthquake in Japan which caused $100 billion damage, most of it uninsured). The problem for the private insurers is that it is expensive to hold huge reserves as collateral against a contingent liability that is inherently uncertain.

3. The systemic risk approach[1]

This approach takes in a holistic consideration of debt: external and domestic, public and private, long-term and short-term, direct and contingent of the country as a whole. For emerging economies, it explicitly recognises the impact of financial liberalisation and capital account liberalisation. It emphasises the rapidly growing financial risks connected with an amplified financial volatility and the systemic effects on the economy. The objective is to measure the maximum downside risks a country can face. It employs the risk management aspects consideration in the asset-liability framework, but its focus goes beyond the government balance sheet, taking into account the total country risk. However, the methodology is still evolving, and there are various ways of managing the full range of risks a country faces at large.

This is buttressed by the efforts of the IMF, as part of its surveillance over member countries' economic and financial policies, for countries to provide regular information on a set of core economic indicators as well as data critical to the early identification of external and financial sector vulnerability. The templates for the reporting of reserves and external debt are steps in this direction in an examination of risks that might be found by countries. The eventual development of the provision of fiscal data is also under consideration. The reserve template can be found in Appendix II.

Implementing various approaches

It needs to be recognised that any framework for contingent liabilities has to be considered as part of government fiscal policy and its associated accounting basis. In other words, it is not a stand-alone framework, but an integral part of government fiscal rules on expenditure programming, government accounting and auditing and fiscal risk management. It also has a countrywide perspective, identifying which risks should be borne by the government and which by the private sector. It is, however, necessary for government contingent liabilities to be determined on a project-by-project basis (e.g. Columbia), but where a series of projects and different activities are involved, a systematic and integrated risk management approach to evaluating and dealing with contingent liabilities is required in terms of better resource management. This approach is not dissimilar to enterprise-wide systems for risk management implemented by many large multinational firms.

The management of contingent liabilities at the government level involves the following elements:

(a) the overall policy of approving projects, activities and transactions that give rise to government contingent liabilities;

(b) the identification, classification and recording of contingent liabilities and risk exposure;

(c) quantifying such contingent liabilities in the context of the budget, whether funded or unfunded;

(d) the provision of funds/reserves to meet contingent liabilities and unexpected losses;

(e) implementing systems for monitoring and controlling government risk exposure from contingent liabilities.

---

1   See Raj Kumar (1999).

The experiences in (e) would feed back into (a), i.e. the overall policy. Management has to be considered in the context of macro-economic developments and forecasts that can affect the probabilities of the triggering of contingent liabilities. External sector liabilities are an integral component of external debt and reserves management. As such, the management of contingent liabilities is dynamic in character, with continuous, or at least, periodic adjustment of values.

The valuation of contingent liabilities

The need for an appropriate valuation of contingent liabilities is based on the premise that given their conditional and time-dependent nature, the provision for such liabilities in the budget of the relevant institution should neither be nil (as is often the case with cash-based budgeting) nor necessarily equal to their full value at the time of the contract (so as to ensure a more efficient deployment of resources). Such a valuation procedure would also facilitate an assessment of the adequacy of banking capital to provide for their external contingent liabilities.

There are several methods to value guarantees (contingent liabilities) and they range from simple rule of thumb methods to sophisticated valuation methods. Experience has shown that the choice of alternative methods would depend on the nature of the contingent liability, the availability of data to measure the risk and the ease to which it could be applied in the budget. This report does not deal in depth with valuation issues, which will be the next activity once methodological and other issues of contingent liabilities are clarified. Some of the most common methods of valuation are shown below.

Rule of thumb

The rule of thumb approach compares the market value of the debt (or the relevant underlying variable) with a risk-free asset and, based on the difference, determines the value of guaranteeing the risky debt. The calculation is approximate in most cases, but it may be the only practical approach when sufficient data is not available.

Market valuation

The market valuation method, on the other hand, compares the prices of similar assets with and without guarantees (based on the fact that the purpose of the guarantees is to lower the interest charged on loans and thus, the value of the guarantee is equivalent to the subsidy in the interest rate). The periodic subsidy to the holder of the guaranteed loan can be measured by the difference in the annual cash flows between the two loan contracts. The full value of the guarantee is the present discounted value of this cash flow.

The estimated probability of default

Another approach to the estimation of the likely financial burden of government guarantees could be to estimate the probability of default by the insured party. In this context, a somewhat dated but important paper by Edwards (1984) may provide some direction. Against the backdrop of the foreign debt crisis of the early 1980s, Edwards examined the extent to which the international financial community had taken into account the risk characteristics of Less Developed Economies (as reflected in the spread of interest charged on loans over LIBOR) while granting loans. The analysis which was restricted to the determinants of country risk, was based on data on 727 public and public guaranteed loans granted to 19 LDCs (including Argentina, Brazil, Korea, Malaysia, Mexico, Thailand and Yugoslavia) during 1976-80.

A pooled regression analysis found that the debt/GNP ratio had a significantly positive impact on the spread, whereas the reserves/GNP ratio had a significantly negative effect. Other variables such as debt service/exports and loan duration were found to be insignificant. The probabilities of default, which were computed using the estimated coefficients of the explanatory variables, showed considerable variation across countries and over time. Information could be collated on the relevant financial characteristics of the insured entities in order to estimate their probability of default and the likely financial burden on the government.

An alternative approach could be to use more direct measures of default potential, such as those used by credit-rating agencies. These agencies categorise project risks in great detail and assign to them a rating that summarises the risk of default. Traded securities in that risk category are then used to estimate the value of risk-free debt and the present value of risky debt of a similar maturity.

Contingent claims models

Sophisticated valuation techniques of contingent liabilities are based on option-pricing models. A guarantee, in particular, may be viewed as a put option (Merton, 1990) [A put option gives the owner the right, but not the obligation, to sell an asset for a pre-specified (exercise) price on or before a certain maturity date]. To see this, let E be the exercise price of the put option and S be the prevailing market price of the underlying asset on the maturity date.

Two possibilities emerge: (i) if S > E, then the owner would not exercise the option, as he/she would obtain a higher price of the asset in the open market. In this case, the value of the option would be zero and (ii) if S < E, it would be beneficial for the owner to exercise the option. The payoff to the option in this case would be (E-S). Combining the two possibilities, the payoff to a (European) put option at maturity can be written as:

$$P = \text{Max} [0, (E-S)] \qquad (1)$$

Now consider a firm that borrows the amount B and the amount borrowed is covered by a guarantee. Let the value of the firm's assets be V. If the firm repays the full amount at maturity, then the amount of guarantee payout would be zero. However, if the firm were to default on the repayment, then the guarantee payout would be given by (B-V) i.e. the guaranteed amount would be reduced by the liquidation of the firm's assets in the event of a default. Combining the two possibilities, the payoff to the guarantee at maturity can thus be written as:

$$G = \text{Max} [0, (B-V)] \qquad (2)$$

It may be observed that (2) is similar to (1). Thus, the guarantee is similar to a put option on the firm's assets, with an exercise price equal to the face value of its debt (B).

The value of the guarantee can thus be computed using the standard Black Scholes option-pricing model. The main data requirements for this estimation process are the value of the firm's assets, the volatility in the rate of return on the firm's assets, an appropriate discount rate and the time to maturity of the firm's guaranteed debt. Appropriate refinements/extensions to the Merton approach could also be made.

Let us take another example. In estimating the value of interest payment guarantees on the debt of 10 highly indebted developing countries (including Argentina, Brazil, Chile, Mexico and Philippines), Borensztein and Pennacchi (1990) assume that all debt takes the form of floating rate perpetuities and specify a random state variable S(t) that represents the repayment prospects by the debtor country. The interest payment guarantee (G) is then shown to be modelled as a portfolio of two put options, with the following value at maturity:

$$G(j) = Max [0, D\{l + i(j)\}] - Max [0, D - S(j)],$$

where i represents the prevailing interest rate and D the principal amount of the loan.

The standard Black-Scholes model to value the guarantee was, however, appropriately modified in this case so as to take into account the stochastic nature of the interest rate (which is the exercise price). The measurement of the state variable S, which depends upon variables affecting the debtor country's economic situation such as random shocks, terms of trade and government policies, policies adopted by creditor countries and the outcome of the bargaining process between the debtor country and creditor banks, posed a significant problem. A measurement of S was therefore obtained using data on secondary market prices for debt.

Value at Risk (VaR)

One of the most commonly used summary indicators of market risk is VaR. Given a distribution of simulated changes in the value of the guarantee emanating from alternative market (e.g. interest rate) scenarios, VaR calculates the maximum amount the institution could lose over a specified time horizon at a specified probability level.

Alternative methodologies could be employed to model changes in market factors such as historical simulation, Monte Carlo simulation and analytic variance-covariance. The methods discussed above are not exhaustive, but only indicative of the range of valuation techniques that exist. Calculating the contingent liabilities of a country is complex and dynamic in nature if the full scale of market values is to be ascertained. Arthur Anderson (2000) gives a comprehensive account of contingent claims (real options) valuation.

3. Country Experiences when Dealing with Contingent Liabilities

The key findings of country practices with regard to contingent liability management

This section surveys the experiences of six countries: Australia, Canada, Czech Republic, New Zealand, the United Kingdom and the United States, with regard to the management of contingent liabilities. The choice of countries was based on the advanced nature of the way they dealt with contingent liabilities and whether such information was readily available. The situation in other countries such as Bulgaria, Columbia and Thailand was also examined, but it was not possible without further investigation to indicate the existing legal and accounting regimes and how such liabilities are recorded and managed. Individual countries differ in the way they deal with contingent liabilities, but all countries share a common set of principles to capture as best they can contingent liabilities as they affect the government budget. (See Appendix I)

In all the countries surveyed, the consideration of contingent liabilities is an integral part of improving transparency in government operations in general and fiscal transparency in particular. Indeed it is tied to a process of bringing in open government so that citizens and outsiders (investors, traders, etc.) can more accurately assess the government's financial position and the true costs and benefits of government activities.

In this survey it has not been possible to ascertain how the risks arising from contingent liabilities are actually managed. But agencies/departments such as the New Zealand Treasury and the General Directorate of Public Credit in Columbia monitor explicit contingent liabilities of the government as part of overall asset-liability management. In any case, the risks associated with contingent liabilities have to be considered as part of reducing balance sheet risk for the government.

All frameworks tend to look at the issue as part of the government fiscal framework, in line with the IMF's guidelines on fiscal transparency. In addition, these countries also publish information on the international investment position and report information on the new reserves template introduced by the IMF. (Appendix II)

Issues relating to the definition of contingent liabilities

While all frameworks spell out the general notion of defining contingent liabilities as costs the government would have to face if a particular event occurs, the precise scope varies, as well as the detailed items that need to be reported. Nevertheless, in all frameworks there is the provision to report published information in the form of quantifiable and non-quantifiable contingent liabilities. Some examples of quantifiable contingent liabilities are loan guarantees, non-loan guarantees, warranties, callable share capital in international organisations and liabilities arising out of legal disputes (though usually within maximum limits).

Non-quantifiable liabilities include environmental contingencies, exchange rate loans and, in some cases, (e.g. UK) liabilities relating to privatisation. There is also an implicit reason for the non-disclosure or partial/conservative disclosure of estimates; for tactical reasons such as "moral hazard" (e.g. arising out of bank failures) or litigation claims against the government (e.g. litigation involving health matters).

The legal regime

Most governments have in place legislation relating to the power to borrow, invest and enter into other financial obligations on behalf of its citizens, and the responsibility to report those decisions to Parliament through budget documentation, and/or other financial reporting. The legal framework usually sets out the maximum amount of new borrowing and guarantees that the Congress, Parliament or the Minister of Finance can approve over a specified period, usually the fiscal year. The authority to borrow is delegated to the Minister of Finance or the political principal responsible for the Ministry of Finance or Treasury, and requires the Minister to be accountable for those decisions to Parliament.

In all regimes, the need to report on contingent liabilities is also underpinned by fiscal legislation, the main Act and/or regulations. The most comprehensive is the Federal Reform Act of USA, whose important objective is to neutralise budgetary incentives, making policymakers indifferent to whether they choose grants, direct loans or guarantees. The conditions for the recognition and disclosure of contingent liabilities are clearly spelt out. The legislative arrangements of the countries surveyed are set out in Appendix I. The regimes delegate powers to the Ministers of Finance on the implementation aspects.

Accounting

As noted in Chapter 1, cash-based accounting systems are not well suited to record and monitor contingent liabilities, which are often treated as off-balance sheet items. One preferred method is offered by accrual-based accounting systems which can capture contingent liabilities as they are created. Within such systems, contingent liabilities can be recorded at face value and the expected present value of contracts.

In the countries surveyed there is a clear preference for using the accrual accounting framework, although the degree of implementation of this method varies from country to country. There are standards of accounting for the liabilities of the government, for example in Canada and the United States. Appendix I explains the degree of implementation of the accrual framework in the sample surveyed.

None of the frameworks actually sets out the valuation methods for estimating the contingent liabilities. Rather, the greatest reliance is on the exposure method. This is to list the maximum exposure or the maximum potential amount that can be lost from contingent liabilities. Thus a guarantee covering the full amount of a loan outstanding would be recorded at the full nominal value of the underlying loan. Such lists are given by the UK, New Zealand and Australian regimes. The obvious limitation of the method is that there is no information on the likelihood of the contingency occurring. Another is that nominal values may not represent market values.

Further research is necessary to ascertain the valuation methodologies that underpin the calculation of the contingent liabilities. Nevertheless, two important elements in measuring contingent liabilities (and indeed other forms of liabilities) are the accrual accounting method and market valuation of such liabilities. Other emerging aspects are the liquidity risk faced and moral hazard, i.e. avoid creating the expectation that the government would guarantee in full all forms of contingent liabilities, in particular those that are implicit.

Recording, monitoring and management

In most of the regimes surveyed, the reporting of the contingent liabilities is set out as indicated in the accounting section above. Further work is required to ascertain, at the country level, how each contingent liability is identified, measured, recorded, monitored and managed.

Furthermore, in some of the regimes it is necessary to evaluate vulnerabilities relating to the financial sector, where liquidity risks are high. In this regard, the information has to be ascertained from sources outside the fiscal sector, e.g. the reporting of reserves, Central Bank balance sheets and private sector potential external liabilities. In other words, the frameworks for contingent liability disclosures only focus on potential government liability, and not on other sources of systemic risks which the public sector has to bear in special unforeseen circumstances as was the case in the recent East Asian crisis and the 1994/95 Mexican crisis.

The conclusion is that in understanding the comprehensive range of contingent liabilities that the government faces, the fiscal frameworks governing them is only one source of information, albeit an important one, for monitoring and management. This has to be supplemented by a range of information and disclosure requirements for the early identification of external and financial sector vulnerability.

In this connection, standards and benchmarks are being developed, taking into account the diversity in country circumstances. While codes for data disclosures in a range of activities are being developed, it will be left to individual countries to establish their own practical framework for the identification, measurement, disclosure and management of a whole range of contingent liabilities that confront the government.

4. Contingent Liabilities Relating to the Government of India's Guarantees on External Debt

The classification and magnitude of contingent liabilities

The various types of key liabilities of the government of India, classified in accordance with the fiscal risk framework, are set out below:

- Direct explicit liabilities comprise the direct borrowing (either internal or external) by the central government to finance the budgetary gap. Internal liabilities include bonds, securities, and Treasury bills issued by the government. External liabilities include loans taken from multilateral financial organisations and bilateral countries.

- Contingent explicit liabilities of the government include central government guarantees given to the state governments, local governments, banks and financial institutions, public sector and private sector entities.

- Direct implicit liabilities of the government include the write-off of losses from the departmentally run enterprises (posts and telegrams, telecom, railways and other departmentally run public sector companies), subsidies given to them or the write off of past loans given to them.

- Contingent implicit liabilities include the capitalisation of weak banks, financial institutions and public enterprises; the write-off of past tax obligations, debt relief, the bailouts of sick or defaulting public/private entity on non-guaranteed debt and other liabilities, and development support to backward regions.

The magnitude of government guarantees on external debt

Under Article 292 of the Constitution of India, the government of India can provide guarantees within such limits as fixed by Parliament. These guarantees constitute a contingent liability on the Consolidated Fund of India. According to the finance accounts of the union government, as of end March 1998, the maximum amount of (domestic and external) guarantee for which the government entered into agreements was Rs1,220.4 billion (US$30.9 billion), while the outstanding guaranteed amount was placed at Rs738.8 billion (US$18.7 billion).

The guarantees included those given in pursuance of agreements between the government and international financial institutions, foreign lending agencies, foreign governments etc, towards the repayment of principal, payment of interest, or commitment charges on loans, etc (Rs331.0 billion or US$8.4 billion as of end March 1998), counter-guarantees to banks in respect of their having issued letters of authority to foreign suppliers for supplies rendered by them on a credit basis (Rs3.2 billion or US$80 million) and performance guarantees given for the fulfilment of contracts/projects awarded to Indian companies abroad (Rs0.28 billion or US$7.1 million).

The government of India provides guarantees on a selective basis on external borrowings by public sector enterprises, developmental financial institutions and, in some instances, to private sector companies. Such guarantees are to be invoked in the case of default by the borrower. They therefore, constitute the explicit contingent liability of the government and have direct implications for the budget in the event of default.

Table 4.1 provides data on such direct guarantees provided by the government for the public sector, the financial sector and the non-financial private sector since March 1994. There has been a steady decline in government guarantees from US$12.2 billion at the end of March 1995 to US$7.1 billion at the end of March 1999.

Table 4.1: Central government guarantees on external debt

	31 March						31 Dec.
	1994	1995	1996	1997	1998	1999	1999 P
	(US dollar billion, end period)						
1. Govt. Debt	55.9	59.5	53.1	49.1	46.5	46.1	46.9
2. Non-Govt. Debt	36.8	39.5	40.7	44.4	47.0	51.5	52.1
3. of which with Govt. Guarantee*: (a+b+c)	12.2	12.3	10.2	8.2	7.3	7.1	7.5
a. Financial Sector	3.3	3.3	2.7	2.3	2.3	2.4	2.6
b. Public Sector	8.6	8.7	7.1	5.6	4.6	4.3	4.6
c. Private Sector	0.3	0.4	0.4	0.4	0.3	0.3	0.3
4. Total External Debt (1+2)	92.7	99.0	93.7	93.5	93.5	97.7	99.0
5. Govt. Debt and Guaranteed Debt (1+3)	68.1	71.8	63.2	57.3	53.8	53.2	54.4
	(ratios as per cent of)						
6. Govt. Debt and Guaranteed Debt to Total External Debt (5/4)	73.5	72.5	67.4	61.3	57.5	54.5	55.0
7. Govt. Guaranteed Debt to Non-Govt. Debt (3/2)	33.1	31.2	25.0	18.5	15.5	13.7	14.4

*   Direct guarantees on external debt provided by the Central Government.
P   Provisional

Source: India's External Debt: A Status Report, May 2000

Other findings from Table 4.1:

(i) Government direct liabilities have declined in absolute terms from US$55.9 billion as of 31 March 1994 to US$46.9 billion as of 31 December 1999. As a proportion of total debt, such liabilities declined from 60.3 per cent to 47.4 per cent during the same period.

It follows from the above that the total debt with government stake (government and government guaranteed debt) declined in absolute terms from US$68.1 billion on 31 March 1994 to US$54.4 billion as on 31 December 1999. As a proportion of total debt, the share declined from 73.5 per cent to 55.0 per cent during the same period.

(ii) The bulk of the guarantees issued and outstanding are accounted for by the public sector (parastatals) and financial institutions (banks and developmental financial institutions in the public and private sector, that borrow for on-lending purposes). Together, public sector and financial institutions accounted for 97.5 per cent of the total government guaranteed debt at the end of March 1994 and 96.0 per cent at end December 1999. The share of private sector in government guaranteed debt, therefore, has at best been nominal.

(iii) Within the public sector and the financial sector, the public sector has been the main beneficiary of government guarantees. It accounted for more than 70 per cent of the government guaranteed debt issued and outstanding at end March 1994. The share was more than 61 per cent at end December 1999.

External debt guarantees by economic sector

Table 4.2 presents a profile of government guarantees by economic sector since end March 1994. The table covers direct guarantees to the public and the private sector entities. It does not cover guarantees given to developmental financial institutions and other financial intermediaries where the funds are on loan, while the final sector-wise utilisation of funds is not available.

The table highlights the growing share of guarantees extended mainly to the power sector (rising from 21.7 per cent in March 1994 to 52.7 per cent in December 1999), and to some extent, the housing sector (up from 3.0 per cent to 10.7 per cent). The shares of the petroleum and civil aviation sector have, however, declined. These issues are discussed in detail in the next chapter.

Table 4.2: Government guarantees to PSUs and private entities by economic sector

S.No.	Economic Sector	(Figures in percentages)						
		Mar 94	Mar 95	Mar 96	Mar 97	Mar 98	Mar 99	Dec 99
1	Petroleum	31.6	30.1	30.1	23.4	21.4	19.8	18.2
2	Power	21.7	26.3	33.6	40.2	45.2	53.5	52.7
3	Civil Aviation	17.2	15.4	9.0	8.8	7.9	5.7	4.3
4	Aluminium	8.2	6.1	4.1	2.8	3.1	0.0	0.3
5	Steel	5.3	5.2	5.1	4.7	4.3	3.3	2.2
6	Shipping	3.5	3.4	3.6	3.3	3.0	1.0	0.7
7	Housing	3.0	2.7	3.1	3.9	6.0	8.4	10.7
8	Petrochemicals	2.1	2.0	0.8	0.7	0.6	0.5	0.3
9	Coal	1.4	1.3	1.5	1.7	1.8	2.6	4.7
10	Fertilizer	1.0	0.9	0.8	1.1	0.0	0.0	0.0
11	Others	5.2	6.4	8.3	9.3	6.6	5.3	5.9
	Total	**100.0**	**100.0**	**100.0**	**100.0**	**100.0**	**100.0**	**100.0**

Projected debt service payments on government-guaranteed external debt

Table 4.3 gives projected debt service payments on government guaranteed debt outstanding as on 31 December 1999 over the next ten year period. The projections do not include disbursement in pipeline and fresh commitments.

Table 4.3: Projected debt service payments on existing government-guaranteed borrowings

	(US$million)									
	2000-01	2001-02	2002-03	2003-04	2004-05	2005-06	2006-07	2007-08	2008-09	2009-10
Contingent Liability:	852	840	1049	734	703	659	614	604	569	515
Principal	494	509	721	463	461	445	424	438	427	395
Interest	358	331	328	272	241	214	190	167	142	120
Total External Debt:	9203	8573	9273	13041	6972	4870	4499	4535	3376	3128
Principal	6383	6119	7063	10165	5577	3711	3502	3651	2682	2532
Interest	2820	2454	2210	2876	1395	1159	997	884	694	596
	(contingent liability debt service as percentage of total debt service on external debt)									
Total	9.3	9.8	11.3	5.6	10.1	13.5	13.6	13.3	16.9	16.5
Principal	7.7	8.3	10.2	4.6	8.3	12.0	12.1	12.0	15.9	15.6
Interest	12.7	13.5	14.8	9.5	17.3	18.5	19.1	18.9	20.5	20.1

Source: India's External Debt, A Status Report, May 2000.

Government policy towards guarantees

The government of India's policy towards issuing guarantees has evolved over time. The policy does not restrict itself to external debt guarantees, but covers all aspects of government guarantees. The earliest guidelines available in this regard date back to May 1969 which prescribed certain criteria for providing central government guarantees. The main consideration stated in the guidelines was that the guarantee should be justified by "public interest". An illustrative list indicating areas that fall into this category was also given.

The guidelines state that the proposal for guarantee amounts to undertaking a contingent liability and should be examined in the same manner as the proposal for a loan. The issues to be considered in this regard included (i) the public interest that the guarantee would serve; (ii) the creditworthiness of the borrower; (iii) terms of borrowings and (iv) conditions under which the guarantee is to be provided. It applied to guarantees to be provided to both public and private sectors.

Amendments have been made to the original guidelines from time to time. The policy towards guarantees has become tighter. The salient features of the policy towards government guarantee are explained below:

The centralisation of central government guarantee approvals

Guarantee approvals have been centralised over time in the Ministry of Finance. Earlier (guidelines issued in September 1986) guarantees given to public enterprises were decentralised and powers to issue guarantee were vested with the central ministries under whose jurisdiction the public sector came. Only cases where the value of guarantee exceeded Rs5 crore (or total outstanding guarantees exceeded Rs10 crore), were to be referred to the Ministry of Finance. However, with effect from 5 December 1994, all guarantees required Ministry of Finance (Budget Division) approval. This was expected to ensure more effective monitoring and management of contingent liabilities.

The monitoring of central government guarantees

All central government ministries were also required to monitor central government guarantees falling under their jurisdiction. A statement on such guarantees in specific format was required to be submitted to the Budget Division in the Ministry of Finance annually. The earliest guidelines in this regard were issued in May 1969. There were subsequent changes in December 1984, October 1990 and July 1993 aimed at more effective monitoring and reviewing of guarantees.

The central government guarantee to the private sector

The above norms applied to guarantees given to the public sector (the parastatals). For the private sector, the same yardstick was applied in the initial stages. Thus, the May 1969 guidelines gave the "public interest" criteria that was applicable to both public and private sector entities. The policy towards issuing guarantee to private enterprises later became stricter. Thus, according to 31 December 1984 guidelines:

"In the case of Guarantees in favour of private institutions, all cases should be approved by the Ministers concerned (Minister in charge of the Ministry as well as the Finance Minister). If the amount involved exceeds Rs10 lakhs in each case (each institution or group of institutions if the same party is connected with it, the limit being applied after taking into account the guarantees already given in respect of the institution or group of institutions) may be considered for being submitted to the Cabinet for approval."

Central government guarantees for multilateral/bilateral debt

As per the Ministry of Finance Office guidelines issued in June 1993, "Government Guarantees would be extended in respect of multilateral loans to public sector undertakings, wherever required by such agencies. In the case of bilateral loans, no guarantees would be extended." Furthermore, it stated "Government guarantees in respect of multilateral loans to the private sector would be given only where (i) the borrower is the Power sector, and (ii) there are adequate safeguards for the commercial risks taken by the Government of India in extending such guarantees."

The guidelines were partially modified in December 1993. It was stated that, "Government guarantee may be given on all soft loan components of the bilateral aid, but guarantee should not be given for the commercial loan components of such aid. However, in the case of the power sector, extension of Government guarantee even in respect of commercial components may be considered on a case by case basis."

Central government guarantees for external commercial borrowings

According to the guidelines issued in June 1993, "Government guarantees for external commercial borrowings would normally not be extended." The earlier approach towards issuing guarantees for public and private sector borrowings was, however, not very strict. The new policy, therefore, is to discourage guarantees in the case of commercial borrowings. This is also mainly responsible for the substantial decline in the total level of government guarantees outstanding in recent years.

The guarantee fee

As per the guidelines issued in May 1969, the question of the levy of the guarantee fee was to be examined by the concerned administrative ministry. Before the introduction of a uniform guarantee fee vide the guidelines issued in June 1993, the government was generally levying a guarantee fee on loans guaranteed by it. However, the rate of fee to be levied was determined on a case-by-case basis.

Guidelines issued in June 1993 introduced uniform guarantee fees on guarantees given by the central government for both external and domestic borrowings. According to the office memorandum, "All Government guarantee in respect of external borrowings would be subject to a guarantee fee of 1.2 per cent per annum on the outstanding amount of principal and interest. The guarantee fee should be levied on the date of guarantee and thereafter on 1 April every year. Such fees would also be levied in respect of guarantees already issued, but still partially outstanding".

In the event of default, the guidelines said, "While reviewing the guarantees annually, Ministries/Departments may also specifically verify payment of guarantee fee. Where the guarantee fee is not paid on due date for the period of default, fee should be charged double the normal rates."

As regards internal borrowings, the following rates of fee on guarantees given were applicable:

Fee for government guarantees given to domestic debt

Type of borrowing	Rate of Fee (per annum)
1. Borrowings under the market borrowing programme approved by RBI	0.25%
2. Borrowings under intercorporate transfers envisaged in the annual plan	0.25%
3. Other borrowings:	
(i) Public sector including the co-operative sector	1.00%
(ii) Other sectors	2.50%

State guarantees

As in the case of central government guarantees, policy reform was also undertaken for guarantees issued by state governments. (See Box 4.1)

Box 4.1: Guarantees by state governments

In the interest of prudent financial management and the credibility of the guarantees issued by the states, there was a need for a guarantee policy for each state government on the basis of certain parameters. Accordingly, the Reserve Bank of India constituted a technical committee of State Finance Secretaries to examine various issues relating to the state government guarantees. The committee submitted its report in February 1999. The committee has recommended a ceiling on guarantee on the basis of certain parameters and selectivity in the request for and provision of guarantees.

The other recommendations relate to the honouring of guarantees: disclosure, transparency and reporting of guarantees; letters of comfort; automatic debit mechanisms; tripartite structured payment agreements; escrow mechanisms for independent power projects; standardisation of documentation; guarantee fees; the constitution of a contingency fund for guarantees and the monitoring of explicit guarantees and implicit contingent liabilities. Following the report, the government of Karnataka passed a Bill to provide for a ceiling on government guarantees. The Rajasthan government has set up a Guarantee Redemption Fund with an initial contribution of Rs1 crore. The central government also set up a Guarantee Redemption Fund with the initial support of Rs100 crore (about US$2.5 billion).

The impact of government guarantees: some empirical evidence

A sample study was conducted on external borrowings with and without guarantee to examine the impact of government guarantee on the terms of external borrowings, i.e. whether government guarantee has led to any improvement in the financial terms of borrowings. For this purpose, the study identified two borrowings by the same borrower - one with and another without guarantee. In addition, the two borrowings were in the same currency, approximately of the same size and not far apart from the point of view of timing. These conditions are necessary to eliminate the impact of exogenous factors (change in the credit rating of the borrower, change in the international capital market conditions etc.) on the terms of borrowings.

The major finding is that government guarantee does not appear to have led to any significant improvement in the terms of borrowings such as rate of interest, grace period and maturity *vis-à-vis* a no-guarantee situation. The main advantage of government guarantee appears to be market accessibility (i.e. accessing certain creditor sources).

The risk of default on government-guaranteed external debt

The quantification of risk on government guaranteed external debt is important in terms of assessing the impact of such risks on the budget. While there are sophisticated risk valuation techniques, a simple study was carried out on the basis of data of the last 10 years to investigate cases, if any, of defaults. The study shows only two cases of near default. The total debt outstanding in the two cases as on 31 March 1994 was about US$12.0 million. This is less than 0.1 per cent of the total external debt outstanding with government guarantee of US$12.2 billion as on 31 March 1994.

The total debt service (principal and interest) for the two cases in 1993-94 was about US$2.0 million. This is again less than 0.1 per cent of total debt-service related to a government guaranteed debt of US$2,025 million during the same period.

If these estimates are taken as a rough indication of default risk on an actuarial basis, the risk is found to be infinitesimally small. While it may not be an appropriate measure for future default occurrences, it can nevertheless, be concluded that the probability of default on government guaranteed external debt has been virtually zero. This is mainly due to a very strict government policy towards issuing guarantees. The policy has also become increasingly strict. Furthermore, the issue of guarantees is mainly restricted to financially viable public sector enterprises.

Contingent liabilities due to the exchange risk guarantee

Another source of contingent liability in the area of external debt is exchange risk guarantee. Even in situations where there are no guarantees on principal and interest payments, extending exchange risk guarantees could give rise to contingent liabilities, which becomes especially important when the local currency is depreciating. Such a guarantee would mean that the borrower could buy the required foreign exchange for making debt-service payments at the agreed exchange rate. Any loss in local currency terms, due to buying foreign exchange at the current exchange rates, has to be borne by the guarantor.

Exchange guarantee by the government of India

The government had to provide exchange rate guarantees to investors in the international market of government bonds to make issues attractive. One recent example of exchange guarantees is that of Resurgent India Bonds (RIBs), which were launched in August 1998 to raise foreign currency resources from non-resident Indian sources. The issuing agency was the State Bank of India (SBI). As per the agreement with the government of India, SBI would benefit from any exchange rate gain on the total foreign currency raised. In the event of exchange rate depreciation, the loss up to 1 per cent per annum on a compounded basis would be borne by SBI and the balance by the government.

The total funds mobilised through RIBs were US$4.23 billion. The bulk of the money raised was in US dollars. Other minor currencies were pound sterling (GBP) and deutsche mark. The rupee-dollar exchange rate in August 1998 was $1 = Rs42.76. The exchange rate in the last week of August 2000 was $1 = Rs45.79. After providing for 1 per cent compound depreciation, which would be borne by SBI, the exchange loss burden on the government of India, at present due to principal repayment liability, works out to roughly Rs9,46 crore. The actual liability would depend upon the exchange rate prevailing at the time of redemption in 2003.

A more recent instance of exchange guarantee is India Millennium Deposits (IMD) floated by SBI during October-November 2000. The total funds mobilised through IMDs were US$5.51 billion. The deposit scheme carries a tenor of five years and is denominated in US dollar, GBP and euro. As with RIBs, in the event of exchange rate depreciation, the loss of up to 1 per cent per annum on a compounded basis would be borne by the SBI and the balance by the government.

Under an arrangement between the government of India and the Reserve Bank of India, a "maintenance of value" (MOV) account has been worked out (in line with the RIB scheme in 1998), which ensures that there is no cash burden on the government of India budget. The government will issue non-negotiable, non-interest bearing special securities without specified maturity in favour of the RBI, to the extent of the exchange losses to be borne by the government under the scheme. The internal liability of the government increases to the extent of the exchange losses guaranteed.

Exchange guarantee by the Reserve Bank of India

The Foreign Currency Non-Resident Accounts [FCNR(A)] scheme was introduced in November 1975 to provide an attractive foreign currency denominated deposit scheme for non-residents. The deposits were freely repatriable. The exchange risk for both principal and interest withdrawn/repatriated was borne by the Reserve Bank of India, which compensated the commercial banks accepting such deposits against the loss due to exchange rate fluctuations. Notwithstanding the closure of the scheme in August 1994, the maturing deposits continued to be a burden on RBI's balance sheet till August 1997.

The GOI took over the liabilities relating to exchange loss on FCNR(A) deposits with effect from 1 July 1993. Table 4.4 gives an estimate of the total exchange losses on account of FCNR(A) liabilities.

Table 4.4: FCNR(A) deposits and losses due to exchange guarantees since 1991-92

	1991-92	1992-93	1993-94	1994-95	1995-96	1996-97	1997-98
Outstanding Balance[1]:							
US$ billion	9.8	10.6	9.3	7.1	4.3	2.3	0.0
Rupees billion	305.8	331.6	291.8	222.1	146.2	82.8	0.0
Exchange Losses[2]:							
US$ billion[3]	1.8	0.8	0.0	0.7	0.7	0.8	0.4
Rupees billion	55.3	25.7	0.0	20.6	24.4	27.6	18.3

1 : Outstanding balance refers to end March figures for the series.
2 : Exchange losses refer to 1 July-30 June, i.e. 1 July 1992 to 30 June 1993.
3 : Exchange losses in US$ terms have been derived from rupee figures using the average annual exchange rate of rupees per US dollar.

Source: RBI Annual Reports

Other deposit/bond schemes which carried an exchange guarantee:

■ During the balance of payment crisis in 1991, Indian Development Bonds (IDB) were raised with a total subscription of US$1627 million. The bonds had a tenor of five years and were redeemed in January-February 1997. The exchange loss on account of IDBs supported by RBI amounted to Rs376 crore.

■ Similarly, Foreign Currency (Banks and Others) Deposits [FC(B&O)D] and Foreign Currency (Ordinary) Accounts [FCON] were introduced in November 1990 and June 1991 respectively with an exchange rate guarantee extended by the RBI. While the [FC(B&O)D] scheme was discontinued in July 1993, the FCON scheme was discontinued in August 1994.

■ Another liability for which the RBI extended exchange rate guarantee was on the parking of funds by Indian financial institutions. The exchange losses on such deposits prompted RBI to provide depositors with an alternative scheme to FCNR(A), Foreign Currency Non-Resident Banks Accounts [FCNR(B)], under which foreign exchange risks were to be borne by the banks based on their risk perceptions. RBI no longer provides exchange guarantees on any schemes.

5. Contingent Liabilities Relating to Infrastructure Investment

Infrastructure investment in India

Historically, infrastructure development in India has largely been carried out by the government because of long gestation periods, the lumpiness of huge capital, high incremental capital/outputs ratios (ICOR), high risk and low rates of return. As the government resources are limited and there are demands from other sectors, the government has allowed, since 1991, private participation including foreign investment in all infrastructure sectors, which were hitherto reserved for investment only by the public sector. However, it may be observed from Table 5.1 that in 1998, even after eight years of economic reform, the public sector still had the major share in investment and value added in mining and quarrying, electricity and other utilities, railways, telecommunications, banking and insurance.

Table 5.1: Sectoral shares in GDP and gross domestic investment (GDI) (percentage) in 1998

Sl. No.	Sectors	Sectoral share in GDP 1998-99	Sectoral share in GCF 1998-99	Sectoral GDI as % of GDP 1998-99	ICOR	Gestation period (years)	Public sector share in GDP	Public sector share in GDI
1	2	3	4	5	6	7	8	9
1	Agriculture	26.6	7.0	1.6	3.6	1	3	19
2	Forestry and logging	1.1	0.3	0.1	1.0	4	10	79
3	Fishing	1.4	0.8	0.2	8.8	2	0	0
4	Mining and quarrying	2.1	2.3	0.5	4.8	4	95	79
5	Manufacturing	15.6	44.1	10.3	4.3	3	13	9
6	Electricity, gas	2.4	9.7	2.3	26.0	6	107	74
7	Construction	5.7	1.8	0.4	0.9	3	16	14
8	Trade and hotels	13.2	2.6	0.6	1.1	2	3	-12
9	Railways	0.9	1.4	0.3	8.3	3	100	83
10	Other transport	4.6	4.8	1.1	8.2	2	18	14
11	Communications	1.5	3.2	0.8	8.2	3	95	83
12	Banking and insurance	5.9	3.4	0.8	0.2	2	63	25
13	Real estate	5.4	8.7	2.0	13.1	2	1	5
14	Public administration	6.3	6.8	1.6	1.5	1	100	83
15	Other services	7.4	3.1	0.7	1.1	1	39	25
	Total	**100**	**100**	**23.4**	**4.2**		**25**	**30**

Note:

(1) The row for agriculture indicates that:

- Agriculture has a share of 26.6 per cent in GDP (Column 3)
- Agriculture has a share of 7 per cent in gross domestic investment (Column 4)
- Investment in agriculture amounts to 1.6 per cent of GDP (Column 5)
- Incremental capital/output ratio (ICOR) in agriculture is 3.6 (Column 6)
- Agricultural projects have an average gestation period of 1 year (Column 7)
- The public sector accounts for 3 per cent of value added in agriculture (Column 8) and so the private sector contributes 97 per cent of value added in agriculture.
- The public sector accounts for 19 per cent of investment in agriculture (Column 9) and so the private sector contributes 81 per cent investment in agriculture.

(2) The rows for the other sectors have a similar interpretation.

The government of India's counter-guarantees for Independent Power Projects

In view of the paucity of resources of the central and state public sector power-generating enterprises, and the widening gap between the rapidly growing demand for electricity and its supply, a policy package to encourage private investment in the power sector was formulated in 1991 and is currently under implementation. The basic objective of the policy is to mobilise additional resources for capacity addition in power generation and distribution. To make the policy more attractive, the tariff notification has been amended twice, offering an assortment of additional incentives to investors, such as protection of up to 16 per cent on foreign equity from foreign exchange fluctuations, clarity on incentives to be earned for performance beyond 68.5 per cent PLF, liberalised rates of depreciation and flexibility in tariff structures subject to certain conditions.

The response to the new power policy has been encouraging. Since the entry of the private sector in power generation in 1991, Central Electricity Authority (CEA) has accorded techno-economic clearance (TEC) to 56 private sector power projects with a total capacity of around 28,850 MW. Twenty-two private sector power generation projects, which do not require TEC of CEA (having a total capacity of 4760 MW) have already been commissioned. However, several of these projects supply a substantial proportion of power to large, industrial consumers; guarantees from foreign or Indian banks have covered all foreign debt invested in the sector so far (World Bank, March 2000).

Under the initial policy package, the Independent Power Producers (IPPs) generally sell power to SEBs, which distribute power to the consuming sector. Since most SEBs are financially distressed and have a weak track record for meeting payment obligations, and there is the non-availability of their and state government's credit rating in the international financial markets, the security package for an IPP was crucial to the success of a power project. As an initial measure to attract private capital into the power sector, the government of India had extended counter-guarantees to state guarantees for the SEB's payment obligations to generating companies in respect of eight, fast track, private power projects under the terms and conditions given in Box 5.1: The details of the eight fast track IPPs, for which counter-guarantees have been extended, are indicated in Box 5.2. These projects are at different stages of implementation.

The counter-guarantee given by the central government was a measure of confidence building necessary for the initial batch of private projects in the power sector. Although these guarantees increase the comfort levels of the lenders in the initial phase, they are also associated with large, contingent liabilities of both central and state governments and may over-expose the concerned governments in future for the following reasons:

- Restoration of the financial health of SEBs and improvement in their operation performance continues to remain a critical issue in the power sector. Under Section 59 of the Electricity Supply Act, 1948, SEBs are required to achieve a rate of return (ROR) of not less than 3 per cent of their fixed assets in service at the beginning of the year, after providing for interest and depreciation charges less the consumer's contribution. In 1997-98, 13 out of 16 SEBs (excluding OSEB) had a positive ROR (including subsidy). Furthermore, only 3 SEBs (MSEB, HPSEB and BSEB) had an ROR of more than 3 per cent.

- Managerial and financial inefficiencies in state sector utilities have adversely affected capacity addition and system improvement. While the SEBs do not have enough resources to finance future programmes, they are also unable to raise investible funds from alternative sources, due to their poor credit rating as a result of unsatisfactory financial and commercial performance.

- The inability of SEBs to pay their dues in full, to Central Power Utilities (CPUs) adversely affects the finances and investment planning of these CPUs.

- Due to political pressure and public resistance, the SEBs generally follow an irrational tariff structure. In none of the SEBs does unit revenue realisation from the agriculture sector cover even a reasonable fraction of its unit average cost, although agriculture accounts for one fourth of power consumption. This leads to heavy financial losses for the SEBs. The hidden subsidy for the agriculture and domestic sectors has increased from Rs74.5 billion (accounting for 1.2 per cent of GDP) in 1991-92 to Rs338.2 billion (amounting to 1.7 per cent of GDP) in 1999-2000 and is projected to go up further to Rs380 billion (amounting to 1.7 per cent of GDP) in 2000-2001 (Table 5.2). The agriculture sector accounts for about 75 per cent of these hidden subsidies for power. The introduction of the proposed national minimum agricultural tariff of 50 paise/kwh, even if implemented by all states, will leave uncovered a substantial proportion of the subsidy provided to the sector, as the marginal cost of power generation is almost four times the agreed minimum tariff for agriculture.

Table 5.2: The financial performance of the state power sector
(rupees billion)

Items	1991-92	1998-99 (RE)	1999-2000	2000-2001
A. Gross subsidy involved				
(i) On account of sale of power to:				
• Agriculture	59.4	225.4	255.8	282.2
• Households	13.1	72.7	78.9	93.9
• Others	2.0	5.4	3.5	3.6
• **Total**	**74.5**	**303.5**	**338.2**	**379.6**
(ii) Subventions from state governments	20.4	78.5	47.1	55.6
(iii) Net subsidy	54.0	225.0	291.1	324.0
(iv) Surplus from commercial sectors	21.7	68.8	60.9	69.0
(v) Uncovered subsidy	32.3	156.2	230.2	255.0
B. Commercial losses	41.2	180.8	207.1	223.5
C. Rate of return (percentage)	-12.7	-27.5	-31.0	-30.7
D. Additional revenue realisation				
Achieving 3 per cent ROR	49.6	199.9	227.1	254.3
Introducing 50 paise/unit tariff for agriculture	21.8	27.4	29.1	27.5

Source: Economic Survey 1999-2000, Ministry of Finance, Government of India.

However, it may be mentioned here that the total installed capacity of the eight IPPs in Maharashtra, Andhra Pradesh, Orissa, Tamil Nadu and Karnataka, for which counter-guarantees have been provided by the central government, constitute only 16 per cent of the total installed capacity by the SEBs in these states. IPPs are paid through the escrow account for which they have the first charge. Therefore, even if SEBs suffer financial problems, there is very little likelihood that the concerned state governments and the central government would have to service the guarantees. But the SEBs need to undertake power tariff rationalisations to make payments to the national power suppliers.

Box 5.1: Terms and conditions for the provision of counter-guarantees by the central government to the independent power producers

Eligibility criteria

- Counter-guarantees are preceded by an in-depth appraisal of the project proposal by the government of India.

- The Ministry of Power has examined the techno-economic viability and certified that the project is essential and consistent with grid management, the cost per MW of generating capacity is reasonable and the tariff and other parameters comply with notified government of India guidelines.

- The respective State Electricity Board (SEB) has signed a Power Purchase Agreement (PPA) with the developer. The cost per unit is fixed, and clearly indicated in the PPA, with adjustments being allowed only to the extent of known and agreed variations.

- The SEB has opened an irrevocable revolving letter of credit for its payment liabilities of one month to the private power company; and to maintain an escrow account to which revenues equivalent to one month's billing of the private company will be credited.

- The SEB has signed and successfully implemented the Operational and Financial Action Plan (OFAP) with the Power Finance Corporation (PFC).

- The management of SEB and state finances is prudent in the opinion of the Ministry of Finance, the government of India and the SEB has achieved a minimum rate of return of 3 per cent on equity in the preceding year.

Terms and conditions

- The government of India is a secondary guarantor, with the respective state governments being the primary guarantors.

- The government of India's guarantee covers energy payment obligations of the SEBs up to a predetermined annual limit.

- In the event of the termination of the Power Purchase Agreement (PPA), the Independent Power Project (IPP) would be covered against foreign debt obligations up to an amount not exceeding the foreign equity.

- Counter-guarantees are accompanied by agreements with the respective state governments to achieve the agreed performance parameters, backed by financial penalties in the event of default.

- The guarantee limits would be constrained by the annual central transfers of plan assistance and taxes to the respective states and such transfers would be pledged against payment defaults by the SEB or the state government.

- The duration of the guarantee is normally limited to a period of 10 years from the date of entry into commercial service, after which the IPP must rely on alternative security arrangements.

Box 5.2: The status of eight, fast track IPPs approved for GOI counter-guarantees

Name of project/state/ promoter	Capacity and project cost	Brief features	Latest position
1. Dabhol CCGT, Phase I, Maharashtra (M/s Dabhol power co-promoted by Enron, Bechtel and General Electric)	740 MW Rs9051 crore (includes cost of Phase II)	Combined cycle power generation plant, imported liquefied natural gas (LNG)/oil distillate Project cost: US$922 million - 20 year PPA with Maharashtra State Electricity Board (MSEB) - Tariff Rs1.24 (US$0.126) per kwh - 12 year counter-guarantee from the government of India for tariff payments by the MSEB, and termination of guarantee (capped at US$300 million)	Phase I (740 MW) was commissioned on 13. 5. 1999. Financial closure for Phase II of the project was achieved on 6.5.1999. Financial closure in 1995.
2. Jegurupadu CCGT, Andhra Pradesh (M/s GVK Industries Ltd.)	216 MW Rs816 crore	Combined cycle power generation plant - Domestic naphtha/Natural gas - 18 year PPA with Andhra Pradesh State Electricity Board (APSEB) - Financial closure in 1996 - Tariff Rs2.40/kwh	Counter-guarantee of the government of India was issued to the project on 4. 9. I996. The project was fully commissioned in July 1997. Financial closure was achieved in September 1996.
3. Godavari CCGT, Andhra Pradesh (M/s Spectrum Power Generation Ltd.)	208 MW Rs748 crore	Combined cycle power generation plant Domestic naphtha/Natural gas - year PPA with Andhra Pradesh State Electricity Board (APSEB) - Financial closure in 1996 - Tariff Rs1.98/kwh	Counter-guarantee of the government. of India was issued to the project on 4. 9. 1996. The project was fully commissioned in July 1997. Financial closure was achieved in September 1996.
4. Ib Valley TPP (Unit A & B), Orissa (M/s AES Transpower, USA)	500 MW US$326 million + Rs.984 crore @ US$ = Rs.42.50	2 x 250 MW thermal power project based on domestic coal Project cost: US$326.02 million +Rs.983.90 crore (exchange rate US$1 = Rs42.50) PPA with GRIDCO - Tariff Rs2.18 per kwh	The government of India's counter-guarantee was issued on 15.1.95. The government of Orissa (GoO) renegotiated the project with the company with a revised capacity and site. As the Ib Valley project was renegotiated by the government of Orissa before construction could commence with a revised configuration of 2 x 250 MW, the project required a revised techno-economic clearance of CEA, which was accorded on 26.2.1998. The Cabinet, in its meeting on 22. 12. 1999, approved the issue of counter-guarantee to the project under the revised procedure.

Name of project/state/ promoter	Capacity and project cost	Brief features	Latest position
5. Neyveli TPP-Zero Unit (NLC), Tamil Nadu (M/s ST-CMS Electric Co.)	250 MW US$262 + Rs.501 crore @ US$ = Rs31.50	Single unit lignite based thermal power project. Project cost: US$261.59 million + Rs501.10 crore @ 1US$ = Rs 31.50) - 20 year PPA with Tamil Nadu Electricity Board (TNEB) - Financial closure in November 1999. - Tariff Rs2.56 per kwh Amount of foreign debt for which the counter-guar- antee was issued on 14 August 1998: US$52.42 million + DM 237.12 million	On 16.5.1998, the Cabinet approved of the issue of counter-guarantee to the project through a revised proce- dure. Under this procedure, the counter-guarantee was issued to this project on 14 August 1998. The project achieved financial closure on 3 November 1999 and commenced construction activities. The firm financial package is yet to be submitted to the Central Electricity Authority with the recommendations of the govern- ment of Tamil Nadu.
6. Mangalore TPP, Karnataka (M/s Mangalore Power Co. Ltd.)	1000 MW US$752 + Rs1581 crore @ US$ = Rs31.50	4 units of 250 MW based on imported coal GOI decided to await the outcome of a case before the Supreme Court before considering it for the issue of counter-guarantee. The Supreme Court gave its judgement on 13 December 1999. Thereafter, the Cabinet in its meeting held on 22 December 1999 approved the issue of counter-guarantee to the company under the revised procedure. The decision was communicated to the respective state govern- ments on 3.1.2000 and a response is still awaited.	The government of Karnataka has communicated the fact that M/s. CLP Power International propose to implement the Mangalore power project (1013.2 MW) by choosing an Indian partner with 30 per cent equity in the Mangalore Power Company. CLP Power International would retain at least 50 per cent shareholding. Other issues such as legal aspects regarding change in the partnership of Mangalore Power Company, amendments to PPA, conditions laid down for GOI counter-guarantee etc. are being examined by GOK. The Tata Power Company Limited, the Andhra Valley Power Supply Company Limited, the Tata Hydro Electric Power Supply Company Limited, jointly known as Tata Electric Companies, addressed to M/s CLP Power International, have communicated the fact that they are in principle agreeable to subscribe to a minimum of 30 per cent equity share capital of the Mangalore Power Company with a role in the O&M of the plant, which is subject to the joint partici- pation agreement being concluded to the satisfaction of both the parties and approval of the Board of the three Tata Electric Companies.

Name of project/state/ promoter	Capacity and project cost	Brief features	Latest position
7. Visakhapatnam TPP, Andhra Pradesh (M/s Ashok Leyland and M/s National Power Plc.UK)	1040 MW US$944 + Rs1325 crore @ US$ = Rs.35.00	2 units of 520 MW based on domestic coal - 30 year PPA with Andhra Pradesh State Electricity Board (APSEB) - Tariff Rs.2.09 per kwh - Amount of foreign debt for which counter-guarantee was issued on 19 August 1998: US$818 million	On 16. 5. 1998, the Cabinet approved of the issue of counter-guarantee to the project through a revised procedure. Under this procedure, the counter-guarantee was issued to this project on 19 August 1998. In terms of the counter-guarantee, the government of Andhra Pradesh/APSEB (now APTRANSCO) is required to forward the firm finan-cial package, along with their recommendations, to Central Electricity Authority.
8. Bhadravati TPP, Maharashtra (M/s Central India Power Co.Ltd.)	1082 MW Rs5187 crore	2 units of 536 MW based on domestic coal - 30 year PPA with Maharashtra State Electricity Board (MSEB) - Tariff Rs2.66 per kwh - Amount of foreign debt for which the counter-guar-antee was issued on 1 August 1998: UK£332 million + F FR. 1480 million	On 16 May 1998, the Cabinet approved of the issue of counter-guarantee to the project through a revised procedure. Under this procedure, the counter-guarantee was issued to the project on 1 August 1998. In terms of the counter-guarantee, the government of the Maharashtra/Maharashtra State Electricity Board (MSEB) is required to forward the firm financial package, along with their recom-mendations, to the Central Electricity Authority.

BOT projects on roads in India

Although India has the third largest road network in the world, transport is neither speedy nor efficient, due to the large proportion of unsurfaced roads (50 per cent) and the overdependence on national highways. The national highways run over 38,445 kms and account for less than 2 per cent of the total road network, but carry as much as 40 per cent of the movement of goods and passenger services in the country. Currently, 85 per cent of the passenger movement and 65 per cent of the freight movement depend on roads. This calls for an urgent need to identify the major bottlenecks on road networks that impede smooth traffic flow. As public funds are limited the government is increasingly encouraging private participation including foreign investment in road construction and transport.

Financing road networks

India has a Central Road Fund and a long history of collecting road user charges through the imposition of excise and import duties on petroleum products and fees and other taxes on road users. Total road user charges account for about 2.1 per cent of GDP and about one third of this amount is spent on state and national roads and highways. The Central Road Fund raises about Rs.200 million for road development, but these funds are retained in the consolidated funds of the central government.

The Ministry of Finance makes an allocation for the road sector. The 1998-99 Central Budget introduced an additional Rs1 levy on petrol. The 1999-2000 budget levied additional tax of Rs1 per litre on diesel to generate about Rs50 billion a year. These funds will be earmarked for the National Highway Authority of India (NHAI) and will be distributed among rural roads, roads, and railways in a 50:40:10 ratio. The road component will be divided among state highways and national highways in the ratio of 35 and 65 and will be used mainly for providing financial support to the private sector to construct highways and expressways on a Build Operate Transfer (BOT) basis. The rail component will be used to construct bridges over railways and safety works at manned and unmanned level crossings.

The BOT model agreement for financing private projects in the infrastructure sector

The government has adopted a concessionaire approach for attracting private sector funds for infrastructure development. Financial arrangements such as Build Operate Transfer (BOT), Build Operate Own (BOO) and Build Operate Own Transfer (BOOT) are being adopted. As in most developing countries, the most prominent and widely used arrangement in India is that of BOT. As the term suggests, the private investor (concessionaire) builds, operates and transfers the facility back to the government at the end of the specified period called the concession period.

The financial implications for the government or its representative organisation which enters into an agreement with a private agency willing to participate in infrastructure investment are briefly outlined below. In most cases the government or the authority representing the government provides the following support to the concessionaire:

Grants

- Cash support by way of an outright grant for meeting the capital cost of the project in the form of equity support.

- The equity support does not exceed 25 per cent of the total project cost and is not greater than total equity capital actually subscribed by shareholders.

- The balance of the grant, if any, is provided for meeting the O&M expenses of the projects.

The revenue shortfall loan

- If the realisable fee in any accounting year during the concession period falls below the subsistence revenue level as the result of an indirect political event or a political event, the concessionaire will be provided with the shortfall support by way of a loan from the government for its representative.

Force majeure events

- A force majeure event means any event or circumstance, or a combination of events which may materially and adversely affect the party claiming force majeure from performing its obligations, in whole or in part, under the agreement. A force majeure event could occur due to a non-political event, an indirect political event or a political event which prevents the party claiming force measures from performing its obligations under the agreement.

- Non-political force measures are acts of God, such as natural disasters, epidemics, radioactive contamination, labour difficulties and contractor failure.

- Indirect political force measures include events such as war, revolution, agitation, industry-wise or state-wise strikes for a continuous period exceeding seven days.

- Political force measure events include changes in law, compulsory acquisition by government agencies of project assets.

The effect of force majeure events before financial close

- The date for achieving financial close shall be extended by the period of force majeure.

- Each Party shall bear its costs, if any, incurred as a consequence of such a force majeure event.

The effect of force majeure events after financial close

- The costs arising out of such force majeure events shall be borne in accordance with the provisions of the Clause relating to the allocation of costs during the subsistence of force majeure.

Allocation of costs during subsistence of force majeure

- Upon the occurrence of force majeure events after financial close and the costs arising due to a non-political event, the Parties shall bear the respective cost.
  - Where a force majeure event is an indirect political event, the costs attributable to such a force majeure event and directly relating to the project shall be borne by the concessionaire to the extent of the insurance claim, for costs exceeding insurance claims, half of the same to the extent actually incurred shall be reimbursed by the government/representative in a lump sum or three equal instalments with an interest rate @ SBI PLR + 2%.
  - In the case of a political event, the force majeure costs incurred shall be reimbursed by the government/representative to the concessionaire in one lump sum or paid in three equal annual instalments with interest @ SBI PLR + 2%, provided that no force majeure cost shall be payable by the government if the concession period is increased.
  - Where the force majeure event is a political event, the force majeure costs to the extent actually incurred and certified by the Statutory Auditors of Concessionaire shall be reimbursed.

Termination payment for force majeure events

■ If the termination is on account of a non-political event, the concessionaire shall be entitled to receive from the government/representative by way of termination payment, an amount equal to 90 per cent of the debt due and the entire subordinated debt less insurance claims, if any.

■ If the termination is on account of an indirect political event, the concessionaire shall receive termination payment equal to the total debt due, less insurance claims if any, plus the outstanding subordinated debt, plus 110 per cent of the equity (subscribed in cash and actually spent on the project, but excluding the equity support) if termination occurs at any time during three years of commencing. The amount will be adjusted to reflect changes in WPI for each successive year, and then reduced every year by 7.5 per cent per annum.

■ If the termination of this agreement is on account of a political event, termination payment is an amount equal to: the total debt due, plus 120 per cent of the subordinated debt, plus 150 per cent of the equity as enumerated above.

Liability for other losses

Except as provided in the model agreement, neither party will be liable to any other party in respect of any loss, damage, cost, expense, claims, arising out of the occurrence of any force majeure event.

Private sector participation to date

The National Highways Act has been amended to enable the levy of a toll on selected sections of national highways so that private participation in road construction on a Build Operate Transfer (BOT) basis can be facilitated. This will complement the efforts of the Public Works Departments. The measures formulated to encourage private sector participation in the road sector, include permission for the National Highways Authority of India (NHAI) to fund equity in private or public companies.

The government of India/NHAI will also consider providing cash support for selected projects. The Ministry of Finance has decided to assume 80 per cent debt service liabilities of the NHAI for the external loans from multilateral agencies, while the NHAI will service the rest of the external debt. The World Bank has already approved a US$516 million loan for four sectors ranging the 477 km long Agra-Calcutta stretch of the national highway. In the case of BOT projects, the government will compensate entrepreneurs according to international norms in those cases where the collection of tolls is hampered by either force majeure or policy risks as discussed above. So far, 20 BOT projects with an estimated cost of more than Rs1020 crore (about US$250 million) have been approved (Details are given in Box 5.3).

Land acquisition procedures have been streamlined and land use policies have been liberalised to enable private investors to develop highway-related facilities enroute such as restaurants, motels and rest/parking areas. The NHAI and in some cases the State Public Works Departments will also assist private entrepreneurs to acquire and commercialise land for the establishment of transport cities, cargo terminals, warehouses/godowns, vehicle repair facilities, shops for vehicle components and parts. The liberalisation of foreign investment norms in the road sector has resulted in the granting of automatic approvals for foreign equity participation up to 74 per cent in the construction and maintenance of roads and bridges, and up to 51 per cent in supporting services to land transport such as the operation of highway bridges, toll roads and vehicular tunnels.

Box 5.3: BOT projects on roads

SL No.	Project Name/ State	NH No.	Length in Km	Cost in Rupees Crore	Conces- sion Period	Construc- tion Period	Dates of Signing/ Completion	Type of Vehicles Tolled	Fee rates Rs/trip
1.	Thane-Bhiwandi Bypass * Maharashtra	3&4	24	103	18 yrs 6 m	36m	9.12.95 31.12.2001	Cars/vans Trucks	10 30
2.	Chalthan Road Over Bridge * Gujarat	8	14	10	41 m 22 d	18 m	19.09.96 15.07.1998	Cars/vans Trucks/Buses	5 15
3.	Udaipur Bypass * Rajasthan	8	11	24	11 yr 8 m	18 m	July 96 22.04.1998	Cars/vans Buses	6 15
4	Construction of six bridges Andhra Pradesh	5	6	50	19 yrs 60 days	4 yrs	9.04.97 8.06.2001	Cars/Jeeps Buses/Trucks & Autoriksha	5 15 2
5.	Coimbatore Bypass Tamil Nadu	47	33	90	32 yrs	24 m	3.10.1997 3.12.1999	Car/Jeeps LCVs Buses	19 28 56
6.	Durg Bypass Madhya Pradesh	6	18.4	68	32 yrs 6 m	30 m	5.11.1997 5.05.2000	Car/Jeeps LCVs/ MAVs Buses/Trucks	 50
7.	Narmada bridge Gujarat	8	6	113	15 yrs	3 yrs	21.11.1997 21.12.2000	Truck/Bus LCV/ Car	33
8.	Nardhana ROB Maharashtra	3	13	34.21	15 yrs 10 m	3 yrs	25.11.1997 25.11.2000	Truck/Bus Trailer/Car	30/25 80/8
9.	Patalganga Bridge Maharashtra	17	1	33.3	17 yrs 9 m	2 yrs 9 m	29.11.1997 29.08.2001	Truck Trailer Truck/bus	50 30
10.	Hubli-Dharwar Bypass Karnataka	4	30.35	68	26 yrs	3 yrs 6 m	5.02.1998 5.11.2001	Car/Jeep/Van Bus/Truck LCV/MAV	10 35/40 25/40
11.	Ndellor Bypass Andhra Pradesh	5	18	73	31 yrs 6 m	30 m	17.02.1998 17.02.2001	Car/Jeep/Van Bus/Truck LCV/ MAV	24 36/48 15/60
12.	Koratalaiyar Bridge Tamil Nadu	5		30	9 yrs 11 m & 16 d	24 m	28.10.1998 Oct., 2000	Car/Jeep/Van LCV Truck/bus MAV/MCM/EME	8 15 30 40
13.	Khambatki Ghat tunnel & road Maharastra	4	8	37.8	9 yrs 9 m	24 m	16.11.1998 Nov., 2000	Car/Jeep Truck/bus Trailer	10 30 50

SL No.	Project Name/ State	NH No.	Length in Km	Cost in Rupees Crore	Conces- sion Period	Construc- tion Period	Dates of Signing/ Completion	Type of Vehicles Tolled	Fee rates Rs/trip
14.	Maharashtra				11 m		Nov. 1999	Bus Truck Trailer	15/20/25 20/25/30 30/35/40
15.	Wainganga Bridge Maharashtra	6	530	32.6	18 yrs 9 m	30 m	16.11.1998 May 2001	Car/Jeep Bus Truck Trailer	10 50 50 80
16.	Mahi Bridge Gujarat	8		42	7 yrs 8 m	18 m	16.11.1998 July 2000	Car/Jeep/Van LCV Truck/bus MAV/MCM	10 20 35 75
17.	ROB Kishangrah Bypass Rajasthan	8	1	16.66	51 m	15 m	27.11.1998 25.04.2000	Car/Jeep/Van LCV Truck/bus MAV/MCM	20 30 40 60
18.	Bridge across river Watrak Gujarat	8		48.2		42 m	1.03.1999 31.12.2002	Car/Jeep/Van LCV Truck/bus MAV/MCM	10 20 35 75
19.	Moradabad Bypass, Uttar Pradesh	24	18	100		30 m	23.04.1999 23.10.2001	Car/Jeep/Van Bus Truck LCV/ MAV	25 35 48 15/60
20.	Derabasi ROB Punjab	22		35.76			8.09.1999		
	Total			**1019.98**					

Contingent liabilities for telecommunications

The Department of Telecommunications has communicated the fact that explicit contingent liabilities include telecom bonds issued by MTNL for partly financing the development needs of the Department of Telecom Services (DTS). These bonds are guaranteed by the Ministry of Finance on payment of a guarantee fee @ 1 per cent per annum. The sum guaranteed and outstanding as on 31 March 2000 was Rs30.2 billion. On the same date, the implicit liabilities amounted to Rs11.2 billion due to the default of repayments of principal and payments of interest charges on account of lease and deferred payment equipment financing contracts.

Contingent liabilities for ports

The government has also undertaken BOT projects on ports based on a model BOT concession agreement for ports. Build Own Operate and Transfer (BOOT) projects by the private sector have been finalised for the construction of a berth at Mumbai and the construction of two multi-purpose bulk cargo berths at Mormagao, and BOT projects have been finalised for the construction of a container terminal at INPT, Navi Mumbai, and the construction of two berths at Vishakapatnam Port. At Chennai, the Central Government has given counter-guarantees for the modernisation of the East and West Highway and extension of the North and South Highway.

Overall recommendations

The overall recommendations concerning contingent liability management have been set out in the last chapter. With regard to specific recommendations relating to infrastructure investment, the World Bank has made a number of recommendations (Boxes 5.4 and 5.5) with which we agree in principle.

Box 5.4: Managing contingent liabilities: World Bank recommendations

In "Country Framework Report for Private Participation in Infrastructure in India" World Bank (March 2000) various measures for containing the government's contingent liabilities have been suggested. We particularly agree with the following measures:

Reporting and Valuing Contingent Liabilities
There is growing concern about the potential level of contingent liabilities that state governments are incurring as more infrastructure projects reach financial closure. As the number of privately-funded infrastructure projects increases, there will be a greater need for state governments to monitor their contingent liabilities systematically. State governments now report guarantees to the state legislature. However, letters of comfort, which are not legally binding, but represent a strong statement of commitment, are not required to be reported. The government of Andhra Pradesh does report these "softer" contingent liabilities. In addition to measuring their liabilities, public agencies need to create liquid funds that will allow agencies to meet liabilities as they arise, rather than wait for the next annual budget cycle.

Auditing Public Support to Private Infrastructure Projects
Given the substantial support that public-private infrastructure partnerships are likely to receive from the government, India should work toward establishing capabilities to audit the award of these projects. The goal would be to assure the public that the government had achieved value for money. In the United Kingdom, the National Audit Office supplements its own skills with those of professional advisors, including lawyers, investment bankers, and accountants. Skills within government units in India could be augmented through a similar system.

Power
Privatise the power sector
■ Make distribution the priority for privatisation. The corporatisation of SEBs, while a necessary starting point, is unlikely to produce the conditions required for improving performance and stopping the theft of power.

- Introduce comprehensive legislation that transfers state electricity board assets to successor companies, outlines the new industry structure, and creates regulators with appropriate powers as the starting point for privatisation.

Roads

Monitor and gradually reduce public support for private road projects

Review the need for certain forms of public sector support for roads, such as covering senior debt in the event of a concessionaire default, following the first phase of successful concessions. In addition, develop public sector support mechanisms that are well targeted and easy for the government to monitor.

Establish incentive structures and demand risk in road concessions

- Consider establishing a system for the government to award projects on the basis of the lowest present value of gross revenues at a concession auction. The concessioning authority would set toll and discount rates, and the concession would not have a fixed term, but would end when the concessionaire earns what it bid.

- Establish a measurable value of the concession to simplify issues related to compensation for early termination.

- Consider other countries' approaches to public support for privately funded road projects.

- Shadow tolls: a capacity payment is made as long as the concessionaire complies with certain key technical or social parameters. The capacity payment can be sized to cover a certain proportion of the project's fixed costs, or it can be a variable payment based on actual usage by vehicle type (the greater the weight on the variable payment, the lower the governments exposure to demand risk).

- Toll road utility: project financing is converted into corporate financing once several projects are operating successfully.

Establish efficient award criteria for concessions

- When competition in the market is strong, the government would take bids on the highest price paid for the assets or shares of the enterprise being privatised, the highest concession fee (one-time), or the highest net present value of discounted revenue streams over the concession period to accrue to the government.

- When competition in the market is weak or non-existent, the government would be alert to the risk of rent-seeking behaviour, and therefore take bids on the basis of the lowest tariff charged to consumers.

Box 5.5: Managing contingent liabilities in infrastructure

In a paper entitled "Managing a Guarantee Programme in Support of Infrastructure Investment" Michael Kleen, also from the World Bank has recommended very similar measures to minimise contingent liabilities on the government for private infrastructure projects. The following are particularly relevant for India:

Recommendation (1): The decision to grant a guarantee should be based on an explicit cost-benefit analysis for the project to be guaranteed, including an assessment of the likely cost to taxpayers and the impact of alternative forms of government support.

Recommendation (2): In principle, when the rationale for government support arises from the difference between effective private willingness to pay and social benefits, it should take the form of subsidies supplementing the price customers are willing to pay for a service. Such subsidies are contingent on the effective provision of the subsidised service. They allow the private provider to be guided by the full benefits of the project without lowering incentives to perform, as would be the case under some form of risk-sharing via co-financing or guarantee.

Recommendation (3): Guarantees of "policy" risks should support a credible reform programme, but not substitute for it. In the medium-term, policy reform should obviate the need for a guarantee. Beneficiaries of guarantees should bear a part of the risk, like a deductible. In structuring guarantees the government needs to take care that performance incentives for private investors are not undermined, essentially by not covering "normal business risk", including exchange rate and interest rate movements.

Recommendation (4): Government risk-sharing in normal business risks should only be considered as a last resort, if at all. To prevent excessive government exposure, decisions should be transparent and based on explicit cost-benefit analysis. Certain forms of support that severely expose the taxpayer, for example, equity investment by the government should either be prohibited or subject to various principles (for example, "buy no more than 25 per cent of the equity"; "require minimum capital at risk of 40 per cent of total assets"). Monetary limits should be placed on total government exposure. There should be an exit strategy for the government, wherever possible.

Recommendation (5): The government should consider creating a central office, which is charged with structuring guarantees so as to minimise taxpayer exposure and to strengthen private performance incentives. Such an agency should be established at arms length from project promoters both within and outside the government. The government should clearly circumscribe the types of guarantee coverage that such an agency may offer. If the government wanted to pursue a significant pipeline of private infrastructure projects it should seriously consider establishing a guarantee corporation, which would help develop standardised guarantee products, facilitate learning across projects, reduce the need for state and municipalities to issue guarantees, allow the employment of competent staff to do so and limit taxpayer exposure in a relatively transparent way.

Recommendation (6): To enable the government to manage its guarantee exposure, it should consider valuing guarantees with their subsidy equivalent and assessing the fiscal impact on that basis, that is, by accrual rather than cash accounting.

Recommendation (7): The government should establish a system to update the valuation of its guarantee exposure periodically, together with mechanisms to adjust guarantee fees or to seize collateral in case fees are not paid as adjusted. In addition, the use to which guarantees can be put should be clearly limited and policies for appropriate guarantee fees and co-insurance requirements established.

6. Contingent Liabilities Relating to Banking, Financial Institutions and the Corporate Sectors of India

In the Indian context, in addition to the government liabilities set out in Chapters 4 and 5, contingent external liabilities relate to three broad sectors: (i) the banking system, (ii) financial institutions and (iii) the corporate sector.

The banking system

Given the gradual process of capital account liberalisation in India, external liabilities that can be incurred by banks are subject to the Reserve Bank's regulations, which involve the specification of capital, gap, reserve and open position requirements. The important sources of contingent external liabilities that can arise in the Indian context, together with some of the specific prudential and reporting requirements are highlighted below.

1. Guarantees extended by Authorised Dealers (ADs) are the major source of contingent liability.

(a) ADs are permitted to extend performance bonds or guarantees in favour of overseas buyers on account of bona fide exports from India. They are also allowed to issue counter-guarantees in favour of their branches/correspondents abroad to cover guarantees required to be issued by the latter on behalf of Indian exporters in cases where guarantees of only resident banks are acceptable to overseas buyers.

(b) ADs can issue guarantees, subject to the prior approval of the Reserve Bank, in favour of foreign lenders or suppliers in the case of external commercial borrowings (ECBs) of residents.

(c) Letters of credit issued by banks to their importer clients are another source of contingent liability. In the case of default by importers, the liability would have to be borne by the banks. However, this would mean that liability would merely transfer from the importer client to the bank, i.e. from one resident to another resident. In other words, this would not result in any incremental liability for the country. Nevertheless, there would be domestic liquidity management issues.

(d) ADs are allowed to give guarantees on behalf of their customer/branch/correspondent outside India in respect of missing or defective documents or authenticity of signatures.

(e) ADs are permitted to give guarantees in favour of organisations outside India issuing travellers' cheques stocked for sale in India by the ADs or by their constituents who are authorised persons.

Some guarantees extended by ADs to non-residents could have an incremental impact on the country's external liabilities.

2. As far as derivative products are concerned, under the current regulations, ADs are allowed to offer forward cover only to the following selected non-residents:

(a) Overseas investors on account of the remittances of dividends in respect of their direct foreign investment in India.

(b) Investments of FIls in debt instruments.

(c) Investments of FIls in equity markets to the extent of 15 per cent of their outstanding investment at end March 1999 and the entire amount of any additional investment over end March 1999. As a measure of flexibility to such FIls who have exhausted the above limits, further limits in excess of 15 per cent are allowed on a case-by-case basis to avoid the building up of large unutilised positions, so as to reduce the risk arising from the volatility in the forex markets. Banks are required to report the facilities provided to FIls on a monthly basis. Available information indicates that this facility has not been much used so far.

(d) NRI deposit holders to the extent of their balances in FCNR(B) and NR(E)R accounts. (See details in Chapter 4)

All these underlying transactions are already reflected in the external liabilities of the recipient country and hence, derivatives would not have any incremental impact.

The Central Bank also intervenes in the forward segment of the forex market. While these transactions between two domestic entities (viz the Central Bank and ADs) would not have any impact on the country's total external liabilities, these could have implications for their respective reserves/capital base. Hence, there is a need to monitor and quantify the risk exposure of such derivative transactions.

3. Non-Resident (NRI) deposits constitute the major share of the external liabilities of the banking system. Within the NRI deposits, two broad categories can be distinguished: rupee denominated deposits and foreign currency denominated deposits.

■ In the case of rupee deposits [(NR(E)R and NR(NR)RD], the banks do not face any currency risk as these liabilities are similar to domestic liabilities.

■ Foreign currency denominated deposits [FCNR (B)] are, however, prone to currency risk (depending on the deployment of the funds) which is borne by banks. The outright sale of foreign currency funds into Indian rupees which could impose an exchange risk and expose banks to open positions, are, however, subject to overall open position limits (as discussed later). Moreover, in the absence of fully developed swap markets, banks may find it difficult to convert these funds into rupees and hence may refrain from deploying these funds in the domestic market. In view of this, the Reserve Bank has allowed Authorised Dealers (ADs) to (a) keep these funds abroad and invest them in foreign currency treasury bills and/or with banks abroad (b) make foreign currency loans to residents for meeting their working capital/capital expenditure requirements. Available survey information indicates that the bulk of the funds under the scheme continue to be held abroad. Thus, a substantial part of foreign currency denominated FCNR(B) deposits have corresponding assets also denominated in foreign currency which minimises the possibility of liabilities arising solely on account of currency fluctuations.

In any case, since FCNR (B) deposits already form part of direct external liabilities, the "contingent" element would not matter from the point of view of direct external liability.

Banks dealing in foreign exchange business are liable to incur currency mismatches as a part of their regular business activities (current account transactions, etc). To discourage banks from taking large positions in assets that would lead to potential losses in the case of strong adverse movements in exchange rates, or need to be sold at significant losses in distress times which could have implications for the solvency of banks, the following prudential requirements have been imposed.

ADs are required to fix their overnight open position limit with the approval of the Reserve Bank. Under the existing regulations, the overall net open position of a bank is calculated on the basis of the internationally accepted "shorthand method". According to the shorthand method, the overall net open position is the higher of the sum of the net short positions of each currency, or the sum of the net long positions of each currency[2]. Until recently, banks were required to maintain on an ongoing basis, Tier II capital at 5 per cent of the open position limit approved by the Reserve Bank. However, this stipulation of an additional capital requirement of 5 per cent of the foreign exchange open position limit, as the Report of the Committee on Banking Sector Reforms (Chairman: Shri M. Narasimham) noted, was not the normal practice in international banking and appeared to be ad hoc. Accordingly, to integrate these risks into the calculation of risk-weighted assets, effective end March 1999, the open positions carry a 100 per cent risk weight. These positions are monitored through a weekly statement called POS.

In addition to the monitoring of the banks' net positions, the ADs are required to monitor their mismatches by fixing suitable gap limits for each currency. The aggregate of such limits fixed by the banks are required to be approved by the Reserve Bank. These limits are monitored by the Reserve Bank through a monthly statement.

Interest sensitivity of banks' external liabilities is monitored through a quarterly statement. While exchange losses arising on account of regular business transactions would not have an impact on direct external liabilities of the economy, these have, as outlined earlier, implications for the capital base of commercial banks.

---

2   The "shorthand method", which has been recommended by the Basle Committee and European Union, is a compromise between the other measures, viz. "gross aggregate position" (the sum of all open positions, both short and long) and "net aggregate position" (the difference between the sum of all long positions and all short positions). The appropriate summary measure would depend upon the correlation among exchange rate changes between the currencies in which a bank holds open positions. Perfect correlation between exchange rate movements would suggest the use of the "net aggregate measure" while complete uncorrelation would suggest the "gross aggregate measure" (Folkerts-Landau and Undgren, 1998).

Financial institutions[3]

The Financial Institutions (FIs) have of late, been increasingly involved with off-balance sheet activities such as extending guarantees, LoCs, financial and project consultancies, etc. Contingent liabilities incurred by FIs arise in the context of performance and loan guarantees, forward exchange contracts, underwriting commitments, uncalled liability on partly-paid investments, claims on the banks not acknowledged as debts, bills for collection, participation certificates, bills discounted and rediscounted, disputed income tax, interest tax, penalty and interest demands.

During the financial year ending March 1999, contingent liabilities as a proportion of the total liabilities/assets worked out as 6.4 per cent in respect of IDBI, 8.7 per cent for ICICI, 11.8 per cent in the case of IFCI and 19.0 per cent for the EXIM Bank. As mentioned earlier, the impact of such liabilities at the national level would depend on the extent to which the "underlying" transaction is already reflected in direct external liabilities of the country. See Box 6.1 for details regarding the EXIM Bank.

Box 6.1: Contingent liabilities of the EXIM Bank of India

The EXIM Bank of India has been playing an important role in promoting India's exports by extending support to Indian companies to submit export projects/contracts in many countries. Towards this objective, the EXIM Bank offers commitments in principle for loans and guarantees. The foreign trade related non-fund based guarantee schemes include:

- deferred payment guarantees in favour of foreign/domestic suppliers/lenders for the purchase of capital equipment on deferred payment terms;

- guarantees in favour of commercial banks/lending institutions abroad on behalf of Indian exporter companies to avail of foreign currency loans for a pre-approved purpose; such guarantees may be issued on a one-off basis or through an umbrella credit line arrangement involving separate guarantees from several Indian companies;

- guarantees in favour of commercial banks/lending institutions abroad on behalf of Indian companies for raising working capital/project finance by overseas joint ventures/wholly-owned subsidiaries of Indian companies;

- guarantees favouring commercial banks/ lending institutions abroad to enable Indian companies to raise foreign currency loans for equity contribution in overseas joint ventures or wholly owned subsidiaries.

---

3   The major all-India financial institutions (FIs) include the Industrial Development Bank of India (IDBI), Industrial Finance Corporation of India (IFCI), Industrial Credit and Investment Corporation of India Ltd. (ICICI), Industrial Investment Bank of India Ltd. (IIBI), Small Industries Development Bank of India (SIDBI), National Housing Bank (NHB), National Bank for Agriculture and Rural Development (NABARD), Export Import Bank of India (EXIM Bank), Tourism Finance Corporation of India (TFCI), and Infrastructure Development Finance Company of India Ltd. (IDFC). Some of the FIs are governed by their own Acts, (e.g., EXIM Bank, IDBI, SIDBI), while others are governed by the Companies Act, 1956 (ICICI, IIBI, IFCI).

The EXIM Bank issues such guarantees on behalf of exporters as a complete package under its non-traditional programmes such as EOU finance, export marketing finance, production equipment finance, export product development finance, finance for joint ventures. Such guarantees are issued under cover of the same fixed assets as are available as security for the funded loan facility and thus form part of the complete package.

During 1998-99, in-principle commitments in respect of export bids amounted to Rs25.3 billion, of which Rs8.6 billion was for loans and Rs16.7 billion was for guarantees. Category-wise, commitments in principle for guarantees comprised Rs10.6 billion for turnkey projects, Rs0.7 billion for consultancy services and Rs0.3 billion for supply contracts.

The EXIM Bank has also been extending lines of credit to overseas financial institutions. Outstanding loans to financial institutions outside India amounted to Rs. 0.05 billion as at end March 1999. Information on the undrawn portion of such loans are, however, not available.

The corporate sector

In accordance with the current exchange control regulations, Indian companies are allowed to provide guarantees in respect of debt or other obligations to non-residents only with the general or special permission of the central government or the Reserve Bank. Some of the important forms of contingent liabilities arising in the corporate sector include:

- guarantees by parent companies in India to their overseas subsidiaries;

- guarantees in respect of external commercial borrowings; and

- guarantees by parent companies in India to their overseas subsidiaries

The policy framework relating to Indian investments abroad has been substantially liberalised over the years. With a view to facilitating overseas investments, Indian companies are permitted to issue guarantees to their subsidiaries or joint ventures abroad. These guarantees are, however, subject to the overall ceiling of investment as applicable to different schemes.

Under the existing rules, Indian parties are allowed to make direct investment in joint ventures/wholly owned subsidiaries abroad via an automatic route as follows:

- Up to US$50 million in a block of three calendar years, subject to specified norms. The ceiling of direct investment will include a contribution to the capital, loan and guarantee. Guarantees given are reckoned at 50 per cent of the face value.

- Without any limit, provided the funding is through an ADR/GDR issue and the total investment does not exceed 50 per cent of the proceeds of the ADR/GDR issue.

- Indian companies engaged in specified sectors (information technology, entertainment software, pharmaceutical and biotechnology) can invest by exchange of ADRs/GDRs up to the lower of US$100 million or 10 times the export earnings of the Indian company, subject to specified guidelines.

In all other cases of outward direct investment, the prior approval of the Reserve Bank is required.

In all cases, the Indian companies are required to report to the Reserve Bank either directly, or through an authorised dealer, the details of overseas investments in specified formats. Since the borrowings of the overseas subsidiaries are not accounted for in a country's direct external liabilities, such guarantees could have an incremental impact on the actual liability position.

Reporting arrangements

Indian promoters are required to furnish particulars of the guarantees in Form ODA while seeking approval. The particulars include the amount of the guarantee, the name of the overseas joint venture, details of the loan that is being guaranteed and the nature of guarantee. With a view to monitoring the guarantees approved by the RBI, the concerned companies are required to submit a certified copy of the guarantee issued to the overseas concern to the bank and also to report the particulars after effecting the remittance.

The number of guarantees issued by the Indian promoters to their subsidiaries has increased significantly in recent years. Approvals for guarantees aggregated US$235 million during 1999-2000, while the cumulative value of guarantees approved by the Reserve Bank of India as at the end of March 2000 was US$795 million. As the maturity periods of such approval vary from case to case, the outstanding value of guarantees may differ from the cumulative value of approvals. In fact, the actual amount of invoked guarantee has been almost insignificant: US$1 million in 1998-99 which declined to US$0.4 million during 1999-2000.

Guarantees under external commercial borrowings

Commercial banks, by and large, guarantee external commercial borrowings. There are also some instances of guarantee issued by companies. Borrowers are required to provide particulars of the loans including details of any guarantee while seeking approval from the Reserve Bank. Needless to say, as the underlying (guaranteed) loans are already a part of external debt, these guarantees do not reflect an additional burden for the country as a whole.

7. Concluding Observations and Recommendations

The issue of managing contingent liabilities in an emerging economy is to be seen in the broader context of economic development. The approach is to view contingent liabilities as a potential tool for furthering the developmental process. The critical aspect is the more effective management of contingent liabilities. Furthermore, since the origin of the problem was the need to manage country risks on private investment flows; such liabilities need to be seen in the overall risk management framework in the emerging economy. Such a framework should cover both the management of existing liabilities and the future issue of such liabilities.

This chapter contains general recommendations for ensuring the effective monitoring and management of contingent liabilities. Though the report has focused mainly on external sector-related contingent liabilities, the recommendations apply to all forms of contingent liabilities. It is also important for the benefit of the reader to review the general reasons leading to an increase in such liabilities in emerging economies, so that the link with the recommendations could be easily established. The main reasons for the growth in contingent liabilities are as follows:

(a) In emerging economies, governments have been called upon to take up greater developmental responsibilities. Faced with budgetary constraints and inspired by the winds of liberalisation affecting the world, governments encouraged foreign private investors to play a greater role in the process, especially in the area of infrastructure development.

Infrastructure sectors such as power, telecom, roads, etc are key to the developmental process. These sectors also required large investment with long gestation periods, uncertain returns and high risk. Investors, therefore, were concerned about long-term returns, given the country risks that characterise emerging economies. To allay the fears of investors, governments often guaranteed minimum returns on investment, exchange risk etc. Loan guarantees were also liberally extended.

(b) Loan guarantees were also liberally extended. Because it was felt that private sector participation creates incentives for efficient operations and productivity, foreign private sector firms also became more familiar with investing in a country. The risks covered can be more explicitly defined in a guarantee than in a loan. For example, the risk of tariff or demand shortfall can either be included or excluded in a guarantee; and more risks such as construction delays can be shifted to the private sector, so that project implementation by a private firm becomes more efficient than the public operators.

(c) Problems arose because the risks inherent in such contingent liabilities were never properly assessed and quantified. Provision was not made for the possible impact of such risks on the budget either. As a result, when guarantees were invoked, it led to a heavy budgetary burden on the issuing governments. Contingent liability, therefore, became a bad word.

(d) The conventional budgeting system followed by most governments also contributed to the growth of contingent liabilities. In such a budgeting framework, guarantees appeared as an off-balance sheet item. Since they did not appear as part of the balance sheet and resource utilisation statements, they were often viewed as a free resource, which encouraged governments to issue guarantees liberally for attracting private sector investment.

(e) Even in cases where the risks were understood, very often the governments did not bother, because the implications of such contingent risks were to be felt in the long run only and there were no immediate budgetary implications.

(f) The problem of moral hazard also surfaced. With governments willing to extend every support to invite foreign investment, investors sometimes insisted on blanket guarantees. Once they could get commitment for assured returns, the investors sometimes did not seriously appraise the projects and their risk/return profile. As a result, unviable and uneconomic projects were also taken up for investment, which led to situations where governments sometimes ended up paying the minimum assured returns to the investors from their own budgetary resources.

(g) However, there is no fundamental difference between the risks associated with direct loans taken by the government and those associated with government guarantees. If there be a shortfall of demand or tariff income of a project, with direct loans, the government has fewer revenue receipts than expected, and it must use taxes to pay back lenders. With a guarantee, the government must also use taxes to pay out the contingent liability if the primary borrowers default.

If the government takes the preservation of the facility, in both cases, it is responsible for making debt service payments. In some cases, guarantees can be better than direct loans because guarantees can be made more explicit and can cover only subsets of risks, while the rest of the risks can be assigned to the private operators, but the government should make proper appraisal and use discretion while granting guarantees.

In terms of the management of contingent liabilities, it may be useful to consider them in terms of existing contingent liabilities and future contingent liabilities.

Existing contingent liabilities

The following steps are suggested for managing existing contingent liabilities:

(i) Identification of all contingent liabilities is the first step. This should include both explicit and implicit components.

(ii) Measurement of the magnitude of contingent liabilities is the next step. In situations where exact measurement is not possible, some estimate could be made for valuing such liabilities. (Different types of contingent liabilities could also be graded according to the visibility defined in terms of exactness of measurement.)

(iii) Inherent risks in contingent liabilities should be clearly quantified. One cannot manage what one cannot measure properly. Different techniques are available for quantifying such risks. These could be adapted according to the specific requirements of the country.

(iv) Adopting accrual-based accounting for the government balance sheet to capture the real implication of contingent liabilities on government finances.

(v) Making provision for such contingent risks in the budget so that the government is not caught off-guard when a guarantee is invoked. In case valuing risks is not possible, a lump sum could be set aside for meeting contingencies. The amount could be revised periodically based on experience.

(vi) Creating an institutional structure to manage contingent liabilities. For this purpose, it is necessary to create a centralised risk management unit which has the necessary expertise for the identification, monitoring and management of all implicit and explicit contingent liabilities. The unit can also advise on providing, reviewing, and structuring new deals to minimise government risks and the formulation of policies and regulations for new commitments.

Only through a centralised unit, could the combined impact of all guarantees on the government budget be properly assessed. The step would also make it possible to identify the correlation between different types of risk and identify situations where some risks could offset each other (adopting a portfolio approach towards contingent liabilities).

(vii) It is necessary to strengthen the internal audit team for contingent liabilities management.

New contingent liabilities

A pragmatic approach for the future issue of contingent liabilities needs to be adopted. This is important because there is an impression, created by past experience, that contingent liability is a bad word and should be avoided. In reality, such liabilities have to be viewed as a tool for furthering the development process and overcoming resource crunch faced by governments. At the same time, a cautious approach is required to avoid the build-up of unwarranted contingent liabilities. To address the issue, a full-fledged policy needs to be developed. The following views may be considered in this context.

(i) There should be no ad hoc issue of guarantees. A clear and transparent policy towards contingent liabilities needs to be developed, which should also be reviewed regularly in the context of changing requirements and circumstances.

(ii) While framing the policy, it is important to keep in mind that guarantees are a means of encouraging private investment in sectors requiring large investment, long gestation periods and uncertain returns. These are infrastructure sectors such as power, transport etc., which are also crucial for the development process to kick start. By offering guaranteed returns, exchange risk protection etc. the government attempts to alleviate fears about risks that the investors perceive in emerging economies. Therefore, there is a need to identify and prioritise areas and sectors that are key for the developmental process and where private sector participation is important.

(iii) It is important to make provision in the budget to cover such risks. This is necessary to ensure that the government is not caught off-guard in the event of a contingent liability being invoked.

(iv) An important consideration is to look at guarantees in the overall risk management framework available to the emerging economy. Contingent liabilities are to be seen as a means of risk management for the private sector. There are other competing alternatives available, which the government could consider. The insurance sector, capital market and their interface play an increasingly important role in risk management functions worldwide. Some of the risks of private investment in infrastructure projects could be passed on to the insurance sector. This would involve the payment of a premium, which is essentially the substitute for the provision made in the budget for the risk of default.

The participation of the insurance sector also has the advantage that the risks would be properly assessed and the problem of moral hazard would be minimised. Another alternative could be to allow some risks to be parcelled out to the capital markets. There is an interface between the insurance sector and the capital markets and the potential of capital markets in absorbing risks is being increasingly accepted.

Where guarantees are absolutely necessary, it would be better if blanket guarantees for assured minimum returns were avoided. Instead, a risk-sharing approach is recommended, where part is borne by the government and part by the investor. This is necessary to avoid the problem of moral hazard and to ensure that the investors evaluate the projects properly.

Appendix I: An Accounting Framework for Contingent Liabilities: Country Practices

Selected country cases for contingent liability management

Australia

The Charter of Budget Honesty Act 1998 provides for the clear enunciation of government fiscal objectives, consistent with the principles of sound fiscal management contained in the Act, and for the regular reporting of performance against the stated objectives. It provides the general framework for fiscal transparency, underpinned by the implementation of an accrual accounting framework. The first budget under the accrual framework was delivered for 1999/2000.

Under the framework, contingent liabilities are defined as costs that the government will have to face if a particular event occurs. The contingent liabilities include loan guarantees, non-loan guarantees, warranties, indemnities, uncalled for capital and letters of comfort. The budget provides a Statement of Risks, which, among other events that affect the fiscal outcome, specifically include the realisation of contingent liabilities.

The Commonwealth's major[4] exposure to contingent liabilities arise out of legislation providing guarantees over certain liabilities of Commonwealth controlled financial institutions (i.e. the Reserve Bank of Australia (RBA), Australian Industry Development Corporation, Housing Loans Insurance Corporation and Export Finance and Insurance Corporation) and the now fully privatised Commonwealth Bank of Australia. Other substantial non-loan guarantees include guarantees payments from Telstra Corporation Ltd to the Telecom Superannuation Scheme.

The strategies for managing these exposures are aimed at ensuring the underlying strength and viability of the entities with respect to which guarantees have been provided so that the guarantees are not triggered. Similar strategies apply to entities not subject to explicit guarantees. This is achieved through, for example:

- the appointment of specialist boards to manage the entities in accordance with sound business practice;

- specific oversight of the businesses by a Minister with responsibilities set down in establishing legislation, or the Memoranda and Articles of Association in the case of Corporations Law companies;

- general monitoring and oversight of all government business enterprises by the Minister for Finance and Cabinet under Government Business Enterprise (GBE) monitoring arrangements; and

---

4   The Commonwealth here means the Federal Government of Australia.

- where applicable, prudential oversight by the RBA, the Insurance and Superannuation Commission and the Australian Securities Commission.

Other arrangements are in place governing the entering into and monitoring of contingent liabilities such as indemnities and uncalled capital. Uncalled capital is primarily associated with international financial institutions such as the IBRD, the Asian Development Bank (ADB) and the European Bank for Reconstruction and Development (EBRD). Arrangements concerning uncalled capital are approved by parliament and reports on the institutions are provided annually by the government to parliament.

Consistent with ABS standards, transactions concerned with the management of international reserves and the monetary system are classified as financing transactions (and do not impact on the deficits). Therefore, contingent liabilities (and assets) with the IMF are not shown here.

The issue of indemnities and other similar undertakings by Commonwealth agencies is primarily governed by the Finance Directions issued under the authority of the Audit Act 1901 and related policy guidelines issued by the Department of Finance. The policy guidelines covering indemnities have been reviewed and will be re-issued. The guidelines will be prepared in consultation with the Australian National Audit Office (ANAO) and the Attorney-General's Department and will be extended to cover guarantees and letters of comfort (No. 6 of 1996-97).

Contingent liabilities are set out in the Statement of Risk as those that are quantifiable and those that are not quantifiable (similar to the New Zealand system considered later). The quantifiable items include guaranteed loans and credit risk facilities as well as the Commonwealth's guarantees of the liabilities of the Reserve Bank of Australia (RBA). The latter include guarantees on the convertibility of notes to gold and the deposits with the RBA by the banking sector. Also covered under the quantifiable items is the uncalled portion of the value of the Commonwealth's shares in the IBRD, ADB and EBRD.

The unquantifiable items include guarantees in some superannuation schemes, clearing up costs arising from ship-sourced marine pollution, a series of guarantees to Australian Airlines Ltd and in the sale of privatised companies and commercialised state corporations such as the Federal Airports Corporation and Qantas Airways Ltd.

Canada

The Public Accounts of Canada, as required under Section 64 (1) of the Financial Administration Act, are tabled each year by the President of the Treasury Board. One of the documents that is published is the annual financial report, which contains the condensed financial statements of Canada, in addition to audited financial statements and finance operations.

The fundamental purpose of these condensed financial statements is to provide an overview of the financial affairs of the government and the resources for which it is responsible under authority granted by parliament. Responsibility for the integrity and objectivity of these statements rests with the government. Among other financial information, the statements also set out contingent or potential liabilities.

Contingent or potential liabilities that may become actual liabilities in future years include: guarantees by the government; callable share capital in international organisations; claims, pending and threatened litigation; and environmental contingencies. These are similar to Australia's specifications.

A typical statement (in this case from the annual financial report of 1998/99) reads as follows:

"Contingent liabilities related to guarantees by the government and international organisations amount to $62 billion. The total amount claimed against the government for other claims and pending and threatened litigation but not assessed is not determinable. Of these other claims, over $200 billion relates to Aboriginal and comprehensive land claims. The government is confident that the ultimate settlement for these contingent liabilities will be for amounts significantly lower than those being disclosed.

Insurance in force relating to self-sustaining insurance programmes operated for the government by three enterprise Crown corporations amounted to approximately $501 billion in 1999 ($485 billion in 1998). The government expects that it will not incur any costs to cover the claims for these programmes."

The Government of Canada reporting entity includes all departments, agencies, corporations and funds which are owned or controlled by the government and which are accountable to parliament. The financial activities of all these entities are consolidated in these statements, except for enterprise Crown corporations and other government business enterprises, which are not dependent on the government for financing their activities. These corporations are reported as investments at their original cost, adjusted by an allowance for valuation to reflect their annual profits or losses. The Canada Pension Plan is excluded from the reporting entity, as it is under the joint control of the government and participating provinces.

The government basically accounts for transactions on an accrual basis. Two notable exceptions are tax revenues and related refunds, which are generally accounted for on a cash basis; and capital assets, which are fully charged to expenditures at the time of acquisition or construction.

As a consequence, the only assets recorded on the condensed statement of assets and liabilities are financial assets, as they can provide resources to discharge liabilities or finance future operations. Assets are recorded at the lower of cost or net realisable value, liabilities being determined on an actuarial basis. Valuation allowances are established for loan guarantees, concessionary and sovereign loans, and other obligations.

The Czech Republic[5]

The general government includes the central government (including state financial assets and extrabudgetary funds) and the local and municipal governments. The fiscal operations of the central government are governed by the law on budgetary rules and some secondary legislation. In addition, there are specific laws governing individual extra budgetary funds.

---

5   This section has been summarised from IMF "Experimental IMF Report on Observance of Standards and Codes: Czech Republic, August 1995]".

The legal framework for Czech budgetary operations tends to rely more on the principles of handling public funds, combined with detailed instructions and regulations, rather than on high-level codified procedures and strong administrative control. A new law on budgetary rules, however, will provide a more comprehensive fiscal framework emphasising greater transparency and accountability, including improving monitoring and reporting of information on guarantees, tax arrears, equity holdings, and the use of appropriate methods of asset valuation.

While the distinction between fiscal and private sector activity is generally clear, there are several areas where the distinction is blurred, a situation which is common for a country in transition. There are several institutions that were established under the Commercial Code which are not a part of the government sector, but neither responds completely to private market incentives. The obligations of these institutions are either explicitly or implicitly guaranteed by the government, but their operations, which are of a fiscal nature, are not completely captured in the fiscal accounts.

Public availability of information

The MOF releases a substantial amount of fiscal information on its website in a timely manner that goes beyond the requirements of the SDDS.

In Resolution 104, 9 February 1998, the MOF was charged with identifying poor quality claims resulting from the economic transformation, hidden debt funding, and state guarantees. These hidden debts capture fiscal activity that is not already included in the fiscal accounts of the government. This initiative was the outcome of the joint work of the MOF and the World Bank. The government included an inventory of hidden forms of debt in its draft of the 1999 state budget.

The authorities recognised that this was necessary to enhance the transparency of the budgetary system and identify an important component of fiscal risk. Hidden financing has several serious shortcomings because decisions are made outside the regular budgetary process. The government has publicly reconfirmed its desire to take over all hidden liabilities which are on the books of public institutions used to finance the costs of transition (Konsolidacni Banka, Ceska Inkasni, Ceska Financni, and the NPF).

In 1998, the hidden liabilities were estimated to be around 13 per cent of GDP, and the World Bank and the government estimate that they are expected to grow at a very fast rate. There are two types of hidden liabilities. Firstly, there are state guarantees that emerged from government support of development projects. At the end of 1998, these guarantees amounted to 6 per cent of GDP after accounting for the risk associated with each guarantee (16 per cent of GDP unadjusted for risk). The annual subsidy component of these guarantees is estimated at about 1.5 per cent of GDP. Secondly, there are bad assets in the public sector institutions resulting from directed credits and purchases of low quality assets from banks in the process of transition. After accounting for reserve provisioning, it is estimated that the outstanding stock of unfunded liabilities is about 7 per cent of GDP.

The government has taken steps to be transparent about the size of the problem by providing an inventory of its hidden debt, but it has not yet developed a clear policy initiative to deal with the problem. Even in the proposed new law on budgetary rules, control of guarantees is rather limited. The solution must include the creation of a legal and institutional framework that forces proper accounting of the true cost of the government within the budget process.

New Zealand

The government sector includes both the central (national) government and local government. But the two levels of government operate independently in fiscal management and reporting. Local governments do not depend heavily on central government for their revenue. Fiscal operations of the central government are governed by the Fiscal Responsibility Act (FRA) and the Public Finance Act (PFA), and the fiscal operations of local government by the Local Government Act (LGA).

Central government includes the core non-commercial government enterprises (SOEs) and Crown Entities (CEs). The SOE and CE models are templates of organisational governance employed by the government that provide for the management of the government's assets and liabilities. SOEs are structured as private sector firms, they do not receive government funding or pay takes and face the same regulatory environment as private sector firms.

Contingent liabilities are defined as estimates of possible future liabilities that may arise from a situation or condition which exists at the balance date, but which is unresolved when the financial statements are prepared. Aspects that are relevant to contingent liability management are as follows:

1. One of the principles set out in the Fiscal Responsibility Act is the prudent management of risks facing the Crown, i.e. to recognise risk and where possible take steps to manage it. Another principle requires that governments should actively try to reduce the risks inherent in their assets, liabilities, and off-balance sheet terms such as guarantees.

2. The government produces financial statements in compliance with the Generally Accepted Accounting Practice (GAAP) which apply to both public and private sectors. The system is accrual based, but also reports on cash flows.

3. The disclosure requirements as far as contingent liabilities are concerned are:

    (a) Statements of the specific fiscal risks facing the Crown in relation to government decisions, and any contingent liabilities of the Crown.

    (b) Disclosure risks that are material to the fiscal position and actively manage those risks to reduce the volatility in fiscal flows and enhance stability in policy settings.

    (c) All New Zealand public sector organisations account using accrual accounting, which requires that contingent liabilities be disclosed.

    A six-monthly statement of contingent liabilities is published. It is divided into:

    (i) quantifiable contingent liabilities
    (ii) non-quantifiable contingent liabilities.

A typical Quantifiable Contingent Liability Statement is presented below:

Statement of Contingent Liabilities as at 31 December 1999
Quantifiable Contingent Liabilities

	31 December 1999 $m	30 June 1999 $m
Guarantees and indemnities	367	541
Uncalled capital	2,885	2,820
Legal proceedings and disputes	509	464
Other contingent liabilities	1,807	1,610
Total Quantifiable Contingent Liabilities	5,568	5,435

Contingent liabilities of the Reserve Bank of New Zealand, State-owned enterprises, Crown entities and Public Trust Office are included in the Statement of Contingent Liabilities. Contingent Liabilities to State-owned enterprises, Crown Entities and Public Trust Office are excluded.

■ The guarantees and indemnities are explicit obligations of the government and are legally encapsulated.

■ Uncalled capital refers to uncalled capital subscriptions to the Asian Development Bank, European Bank for Reconstruction and Development and the IBRD.

■ Legal proceedings and disputes are shown exclusive of any interest and costs that may be claimed if these cases were decided against the Crown.

■ Other quantifiable contingent liabilities including promissory notes are lodged with the IBRD and IMF. Payments of the notes depends upon the operations of the rules of the individual organisation.

■ Non-quantifiable contingent liabilities include a range of liabilities that cannot be quantified, such as the guaranteed benefits payable by all National Provident Fund Board Schemes and as well as liabilities under the Reserve Bank of New Zealand Act 1989. The government pays to the bank any exchange losses incurred by the bank as a result of dealing in foreign exchange. Under this item are also a range of guarantees/indemnities provided in infrastructure projects (e.g. power projects, housing, and construction).

Source: Government of New Zealand www.treasury.govt.nz

The United Kingdom

The focus on the UK budget is on the total public sector, defined as general government plus public corporations. All government activities are governed by a clear and transparent framework of law. Local government operates within a clear legislative framework which defines authorities' ability to raise taxes and to borrow, as well as the financial support the central government provides to local government functions.

■ The UK Code for Fiscal Stability (which sets out the new financial reporting framework) is given statutory underpinning in the Finance Act.

- The annual budget covers all central operations in detail, although much of the more detailed information on public expenditure is published later in the Public Expenditure and Statistical Analysis Report (PESA) and departmental reports.

The Code requires the following, among other information:

- Figures for key fiscal aggregates to be produced for the two years preceding the budget year and projections to be produced for the two following years.

- An annual statement of the contingent liabilities of the consolidated fund is published in the supplementary statements to the consolidated fund and national loans fund accounts.

- The publication of an analysis of the key risks surrounding the economic and fiscal outlooks. This will include government decisions that have still to be quantified with certainty; other material contingent liabilities and past forecast errors.

- The publication of information on the overall debt portfolio used to finance past deficits in the debt management report each March.

- A legal requirement to publish the liabilities and assets of the national loans fund.

- The publication of an economic and fiscal strategy report (normally with the budget). This report will set out their long-term economic and fiscal strategy, (including fiscal policy objectives), assess short-term outcomes against this strategy; present illustrative long-run fiscal projections (for at least 10 years) and analyse the impact of the economic cycle on key fiscal aggregates.

- A report on the key assumptions, forecasts and conventions underpinning its economic and fiscal projections.

The statement of contingent or nominal liabilities of the consolidated fund summarises contingent liabilities of the consolidated fund reported by government departments, excluding:

- cases involving £100,000 or less;

- cases arising in the normal course of departments' business;

- a small number of other cases, of which details have been supplied to the National Audit Office, where there are considerations of national security, or commercial confidentiality, or where public knowledge of a guarantee could prompt claims from third parties.

The listing of the contingent liabilities is by Ministry/Department. Information disclosed is as follows:

- The legal statute that provides for the liabilities.

- The amount outstanding in the last two financial years. Where no direct figures are available, the contingent liabilities are expressed in terms of a limit (i.e. "up to"). Where liabilities cannot be extricated, the information is returned with an "unquantifiable" tax.

Below is the statement of contingent or nominal liabilities for the UK Exports Guarantee Department.

Contingent Liabilities

Export Credits Guarantee Department Statutory Liabilities Charged to Votes	Amount Outstanding at 31.3.99 £m	Amount Outstanding at 31.3.98 £m
Export and Investment Guarantees Act 1991		
Section 1 Credit insurance guarantees, including tender to contractor cover, also guarantees given to minimise loss, refinancing sovereign debt or reduce interest support costs.	26,389.6	27,849.4
Section 1 Commitment to take out export loans in foreign currencies made:		
a. before December 1984.	42.7	43.7
b. since December 1984.	3,919.3	3,937.3
Section 1 Commitment to take out loans funded by Guaranteed Export Finance Corporation (GEFCO).	1,016.0	1,016.0
Section 1 Overseas aid.	0.8	0.8
Section 2 Overseas investment insurance.	520.4	816.9
Section 3 Guarantees to refinance sovereign debt or reduce/contain interest support costs.	1,297.6	1,363.3
Section 3 Commitments to take out loans funded by GEFCO.	1,166.6	1,144.8
Section 3 Swap counter party exposure.	518.8	709.3

Contingent liabilities in respect of privatisation have been explained as follows:

Statement of Contingent or Nominal Liabilities
Contingent Liabilities

Department/Statute	Nature of Liability	Amount Outstanding at 31.3.99 £m	Amount Outstanding at 31.3.98 £m
Department of Trade and Industry	Statutory Liabilities Charged to Votes		
British Aerospace Act 1980, Section 9	BAe: Liabilities immediately prior to privatisation. The government assumed	Unquantifiable	Unquantifiable

British Aerospace Act 1980, Section 9	ultimate responsibility for any outstanding liabilities of British Aerospace existing immediately prior to privatisation on 18 February 1981.	Unquantifiable	Unquantifiable
	The government would only become responsible in the event of a formal winding up of BAe or an order to wind up the company by the court under the Companies Act.		
Telecommunications Act 1984, Section 68 (2)	The government is liable for certain debts of the Corporation which were outstanding at the transfer date and which are now liabilities of BT plc. In the event of British Telecom plc being wound up, other than for the purpose of reconstruction or amalgamation, the government would become liable to pay the company's debts to creditors in respect of obligations which were formerly those of British Telecommunications Corporation and were transferred to British Telecom plc.	Unquantifiable	Unquantifiable

The United States of America

With the introduction of the Federal Credit Reform Act of 1990 (effective for the fiscal year of 1992), the US federal government replaced a parallel budgeting system for contingent liabilities with new budgetary rules for direct and guaranteed loans. These provisions are designed to neutralise budgetary incentives, making policymakers indifferent to whether they choose grants, direct loans or guarantees. The primary interest is to ensure that subsidy costs of direct loans and guarantees are taken into account in budgetary discussions.

The standards for accounting for liabilities, including contingent liabilities are set out in the statement of federal financial accounting standards, Accounting for Liabilities of the Federal Government (September 1995) published by the President Office of Management and Budget. These standards apply to general-purpose financial reports to US Government reporting entities.

The Act has the following specific purposes:

■ to ensure a timely and accurate measure and presentation in the President's budget of the costs of direct loan and loan guarantee programmes;

- to place the cost of credit programmes on a budgetary basis equivalent to other federal spending;

- to encourage the delivery of benefits in the form most appropriate to the needs of beneficiaries; and

- to improve the allocation of resources among credit programmes and between credit and other spending programmes.

The major provisions of the Act :

- require that for each fiscal year in which the direct loans or the loan guarantees are to be obligated, committed, or disbursed, the President's budget reflects the long-term cost to the government of the subsidies associated with the direct loans and loan guarantees. The subsidy cost estimate for the President's budget is to be based on the present value of specified cash flow discounted at the average rate of marketable Treasury securities of similar maturity;

- before direct loans are obligated or loan guarantees are committed, annual appropriations must generally be enacted to cover these costs. However, mandatory programmes have permanent indefinite appropriations;

- provide for borrowing authority from the Treasury to cover the non-subsidy portion of direct loans;

- establish budgetary and financing control for each credit programme.

The present value measurement basis is also applied to loan guarantees. Before credit reform, as in the case of direct loans, loan guarantees were measured for the budget on a cash basis. Thus, loan guarantees could appear to be virtually cost free, since cash payments by the government were not required, unless and until the guaranteed loans defaulted at a future date.

Under credit reform, the future cash outflows required by loan guarantee commitments must be projected and discounted at an appropriate Treasury interest rate. The present value of the cash outflows is the cost of the loan guarantees. Before loan guarantees are committed, annual appropriations generally must be enacted to cover the cost of the loan guarantees. Direct loans and guaranteed loans contracted before 1992 will not require the above treatment.

Contingencies

A contingency is an existing condition, situation, or set of circumstances involving uncertainty as to possible gain or loss to an entity. The uncertainty will ultimately be resolved when one or more future events occur or fail to occur. Resolution of the uncertainty may confirm a gain, (i.e., acquisition of an asset or reduction of a liability) or a loss (i.e., loss or impairment of an asset or the incurrence of a liability).

When a loss contingency (i.e., contingent liability) exists, the likelihood that the future event or events will confirm the loss or the incurrence of a liability can range from probable to remote. The probability classifications are as follows:

| Probable: | The future confirming event or events are more likely than not to occur. |

Probable: The future confirming event or events are more likely than not to occur.

Reasonably possible: The chance of the future confirming event or events occurring is more than remote, but less than probable.

Remote: The chance of the future event or events occurring is slight.

The following are some examples of loss contingencies:

- collectibility of receivables;

- pending or threatened litigation; and

- possible claims and assessments.

Criteria for the recognition of a contingent liability

A contingent liability should be recognised when all of these three conditions are met.

- A past event or exchange transaction has occurred (e.g. a federal entity has breached a contract with a non-federal entity).

- A future outflow or other sacrifice of resources is probable (e.g. the non-federal entity has filed a legal claim against a federal entity for breach of contract and the federal entity's management believes the claim is more likely than not to be settled in favour of the claimant).

- The future outflow or sacrifice of resources is measurable (e.g. the federal entity's management determines an estimated settlement amount).

The estimated liability may be a specific amount or a range of amounts. If some amount within the range is a better estimate than any other amount within the range, that amount is recognised. If no amount within the range is a better estimate than any other amount, the minimum amount in the range is recognised and the range and a description of the nature of the contingency should be disclosed.

Criteria for the disclosure of a contingent liability

A contingent liability should be disclosed if any of the conditions for liability recognition are not met and there is at least a reasonable possibility that a loss or an additional loss may have been incurred. "Disclosure" in this context refers to reporting information in notes regarded as an integral part of the basic financial statements. Disclosure should include the nature of the contingency and an estimate of the possible liability, an estimate of the range of the possible liability, or a statement that such an estimate cannot be made.

In some cases, contingencies may be identified, but the degree of uncertainty is too great that no reporting (i.e., recognition or disclosure) is necessary in the general-purpose federal financial reports. Specifically, contingencies classified as remote, need not be reported in general purpose federal financial reports, though the law may require such disclosures in special purpose reports. If information about remote contingencies is included in general purpose federal financial reports (e.g. the total face amount of insurance and guarantees in force), it should be labelled in such a way as to avoid the misleading inference that there is more than a remote chance of a loss of that amount.

Implementation

Conversion to the subsidy cost basis has entailed the maintenance of separate budgetary accounts for the subsidised and unsubsidised portions of loans and guarantees. Programme accounts receive appropriations for subsidy costs; financing accounts handle the cash flows associated with the non-subsidised portion. Programme accounts are included in the budget; financing accounts, however, are recorded as a "means of financing" and their cash flows are not included in budget receipts or outlays.

Future legislation

The subsidy cost basis is currently used only for direct and guaranteed loans, not for other contingent liabilities. However, legislation tabled in the United States Congress during 1999 (but not yet enacted) would shift all US government insurance programmes to this basis. The legislation provides that beginning with the fiscal year 2006, insurance commitments could be made only to the extent that budget resources were appropriated to cover their "risk-assumed cost". This cost is defined as "the net present value of the estimated cash flows to and from the government resulting from an insurance commitment or modification thereof". Inasmuch as the volume of insurance commitments is many times greater than that of loan guarantees, if this legislation were enacted, it might have an enormous impact on the budgetary treatment of contingent liabilities.

Appendix II: The Special Data Dissemination Standard and the Data Template on International Reserves/Foreign Currency Liquidity

1. The IMF's Special Data Dissemination Standard (SDDS) was established by the Fund's Executive Board in March 1996, with the aim of enhancing the availability of timely and comprehensive economic and financial statistics. The SDDS was intended to guide member countries that have, or might seek, access to international capital markets in their provision of economic and financial data to the public. It was anticipated that the SDDS would contribute to the pursuit of sound macro-economics policies and aid the functioning of financial markets.

2. Subscription to the SDDS is voluntary, but subscribing members agree to provide information on data categories that cover the four sectors of the economy (national income and prices, the fiscal sector, the financial sector and the external sector). Within these sectors the SDDS prescribes the periodicity (or frequency) and timeliness with which the data are to be disseminated. The SDDS coverage also prescribes the advance dissemination of release calendars for the data components and that the data be simultaneously released to all interested parties. More information on the SDDS can be found on the IMF's website at www.dsbb.imf.org.

3. The original specification of the SDDS included, as a prescribed category, the presentation of information on gross international reserves (reserve assets) with a periodicity of one month and a lag of no more than one week. The provision of these data with a periodicity of one week was encouraged. The SDDS also encouraged, but did not prescribe, the provision of information on reserve related liabilities.

4. At the time of the Executive Board's first review of the SDDS in December 1997, events in international financial markets had underscored the importance of the timely provision of information on a country's reserves and reserve related liabilities. It became clear that monthly information on gross international reserves alone did not allow for a sufficiently comprehensive assessment of a country's official foreign currency exposure, and hence its vulnerability to pressures on its foreign currency reserves. At this time the Executive Board asked the staff to consult with SDDS subscribing countries and with users of the SDDS to determine what might be done to strengthen the coverage of reserves and reserve related liabilities in the SDDS.

    The results of this consultation were initially considered by the Executive Board in early September 1998 and were further discussed, including a review of an initial proposal for a disclosure template on international reserves and related items, in December 1998, at the time of the second review of the SDDS. The Executive Board reached a decision on the means of strengthening the provision of information on international reserves and foreign currency liquidity within the SDDS in March 1999.

5. The Executive Board's decision is embodied in the template on international reserves and foreign currency liquidity that is contained in the main body of the text. In addition to providing for more explicit specification of the constituents of official reserve assets, the template provides for the inclusion of details on other official foreign currency assets, and on predetermined and contingent short-term net drains on foreign currency assets. It is thus much broader in conception than the original SDDS specification of gross reserves assets and establishes a new standard for the provision of information to the public on the amount and composition of reserve assets, other foreign exchange assets held by the central bank and the government, short-term foreign liabilities, and related activities that can lead to demands on reserves (such as financial derivatives positions and guarantees extended by the government for private borrowing).

6. In reaching its decision on the reserves template, the Executive Board took account of the widespread interest in increasing the transparency of information on reserves and related items, but was also conscious of the concerns expressed by member countries about the resource costs of compiling and disseminating more detailed, frequent and timely data and the possibility that this would reduce the effectiveness of exchange market intervention. The final decision reflected a balancing of these objectives and concerns. The template was finalised in co-operation with a working group of the committee on the global financial system of the G-10 Central Banks. The G-10 Central B anks have also adopted the template for use in the data dissemination activities of that committee.

7. The SDDS prescription for the completion of the data template calls for the full dissemination of data on a monthly basis, with a lag of no more than one month, although data on total reserve assets are still prescribed for dissemination on a monthly basis with a lag of no more than one week, consistent with the original specification for gross international reserves. The dissemination of the full template on a weekly basis, with a one-week lag, is encouraged.

Source: IMF (See www.imf.org)

Sample Form for Presenting Data in the Template on International Reserves/Foreign Currency Liquidity

(Information to be disclosed by the monetary authorities and other central government, excluding social security) [1][2][3]

I. Official reserve assets and other foreign currency assets (approximate market value) [4]

A. **Official reserve assets**	
(1) Foreign currency reserves (in convertible foreign currencies (a) Securities of which: issuer headquartered in reporting country but located abroad	
(b) total currency and deposits with:	
(i) other national central banks, BIS and IMF	

	(ii) banks headquartered in the reporting countryof which: located abroad	
	(iii) banks headquartered outside the reporting country of which: located in the reporting country	
(2)	IMF reserve position	
(3)	SDRs	
(4)	gold (including gold deposits and, if appropriate, gold swapped) [5] - volume in fine troy ounces	
(5)	other reserve assets (specify)	
	- financial derivatives	
	- loans to nonblank nonresidents	
	- other	
B.	**Other foreign currency assets (specify)**	
	- securities not included in official reserve assets	
	- deposits not included in official reserve assets	
	- loans not included in official reserve assets	
	- financial derivatives not included in official reserve assets	
	- gold not included in official reserve assets	
	- other	

II. Predetermined short-term net drains on foreign currency assets (nominal value)

	Total	Maturity breakdown (residual maturity)		
		Up to 1 month	More than 1 month and up to 3 months	More than 3 months and up to 1 year
1. Foreign currency loans, securities, and deposits [6]				
- outflows (-) Principal				
Interest				
- inflows (+) Principal				
Interest				

2. Aggregate short and long positions in forwards and futures in foreign currencies vis-à-vis the domestic currency (including the forward leg of currency swaps) [7]				
(a) Short positions (-)				
(b) Long positions (+)				
3. Other (specify)				
- outflows related to repos (-)				
- inflows related to reverse repos (+)				
- trade credit (-)				
- trade credit (+)				
- other accounts payable (-)				
- other accounts receivable (+)				

III. Contingent short-term net drains on foreign currency assets (nominal value)

	Total	Maturity breakdown (residual maturity, where applicable)		
		Up to 1 month	More than 1 month and up to 3 months	More than 3 months and up to 1 year
1. Contingent liabilities in foreign currency				
(a) Collateral guarantees on debt falling due within 1 year				
(b) Other contingent liabilities				
2. Foreign currency securities issued with embedded options (puttable bonds) [8]				
3. Undrawn, unconditional credit lines provided by: [9]				
(a) other national monetary authorities, BIS, IMF, and other international organisations				
- other national monetary authorities (+)				

- BIS (+)				
- IMF (+)				
(b) with banks and other financial institutions headquartered in the reporting country (+)				
(c) with banks and other financial institutions headquartered outside the reporting country (+) Undrawn, unconditional credit lines provided to:				
(a) other national monetary authorities, BIS, IMF, and other international organisations				
- other national monetary authorities (-)				
- BIS (-)				
- IMF (-)				
(b) banks and other financial institutions headquartered in the reporting country (-)				
(c) banks and other financial institutions headquartered outside the reporting country (-)				
4. Aggregate short and long positions of options in foreign currencies *vis-à-vis* the domestic currency [10]				
(a) Short positions				
(i) Bought puts				
(ii) Written calls				
(b) Long positions				
(i) Bought calls				
(ii) Written puts				

Notes

1. In principle, only instruments denominated and settled in foreign currency (or those whose valuation is directly dependent on the exchange rate and that are settled in foreign currency) are to be included in categories I, II, and III of the template. Financial instruments denominated in foreign currency and settled in other ways (e.g., in domestic currency or commodities) are included as memo items under Section IV.

2. Netting of positions is allowed only if they have the same maturity, are against the same counter party, and a master netting agreement is in place. Positions on organised exchanges could also be netted.

3. Monetary authorities are defined according to the IMF Balance of Payments Manual, Fifth Edition.

4. In cases of large positions *vis-à-vis* institutions headquartered in the reporting country, in instruments other than deposits or securities, they should be reported as separate items.

5. The valuation basis for gold assets should be disclosed; ideally this would be done by showing the volume and price.

6. Including interest payments due within the corresponding time horizons. Foreign currency deposits held by non-residents with central banks should also be included here. The securities referred to are those issued by the monetary authorities and the central government (excluding social security).

7. In the event that there are forward or futures positions with a residual maturity greater than one year, which could be subject to margin calls, these should be reported separately under Section IV.

8. Only bonds with a residual maturity greater than one year should be reported under this item, as those with shorter maturities will already be included in Section II, above.

9. Reporters should distinguish potential inflows and potential outflows resulting from contingent lines of credit and report them separately, in the specified format.

10. In the event that there are option positions with a residual maturity greater than one year, which could be subject to margin calls, these should be reported separately under Section IV.

11. These "stress-tests" are an encouraged, rather than a prescribed, category of information in the IMF's Special Data Dissemination Standard (SDDS). They could be disclosed in the form of a graph. As a rule, notional value should be reported. However, in the case of cash-settled options, the estimated future inflow/outflow should be disclosed. Positions are "in the money" or would be, under the assumed values.

12. Distinguish between assets and liabilities where applicable.

13. Identify types of instrument; the valuation principles should be the same as in Sections I - III. Where applicable, the notional value of non-deliverable forward positions should be shown in the same format as for the nominal value of deliverable forwards/futures in Section II.

14. Only assets included in Section I that are pledged should be reported here.

15. Assets that are lent or reported should be reported here, whether or not they have been included in Section I of the template, along with any associated liabilities (in Section II). However, these should be reported in two separate categories, depending on whether or not they have been included in Section I. Similarly, securities that are borrowed or acquired under repo agreements should be reported as a separate item and treated symmetrically. Market values should be reported and the accounting treatment disclosed.

16. Identify types of instrument. The main characteristics of internal models used to calculate the market value should be disclosed.

The experience of the countries surveyed has shown that it is not possible to merely single out contingent liability management without consideration of more broader aspects of government transparency and data provision.

References

Andersen, A. (2000) Contingent Claims (Real Options) Valuation of Contingent Liabilities, Auckland, New Zealand.

Australia Treasury, Annual Report, 1998-1999.

Borensztein, E. and Pennacchi, G. (1990) Valuation of Interest Payment Guarantees on Developing Country Debt, IMF Staff Papers, Vol. 37(4), December.

Dailami, M. and Klein, M. (1997) Government Support to Private Infrastructure Projects in Emerging Markets, Paper presented at conference, Managing Government Exposure to Private Infrastructure Projects: Averting a New Style Debt Crisis, Cartagena, Columbia 29-30 May 1997.

Department of Finance, Canada, (1998) Debt Management Report, Ottawa.

Earterly, W. and Yuravlivler, D. (2000) Treasuries or Time Bombs, World Bank Draft Report, Feb 2000.

Financial Stability Forum, Report of the Working Group on Capital Flows, April 2000.

Finance Canada, Annual Financial Report, 1998-1999.

Honohan, P. (1999) Fiscal Contingency Planning for Banking Crisis, Policy Research Working Paper 2228, World Bank Development Research Group, Nov 1999.

International Monetary Fund, Debt and Reserve Related Indicators of External Vulnerability, March 23, 2000.

International Monetary Fund, Report on the Observance of Standards and Codes: Czech Republic, July 2000.

International Monetary Fund, Code of Good Practices on Fiscal Transparency: Declaration on Principles, April 1999.

Kopits, G. and Craig, J. (1998) Transparency in Government Operations, IMF Occasional Paper No. 158, Jan 1988, Washington.

Kharas, H. and Mishra D. (1999) Hidden Deficits and Currency Crisis, World Bank draft paper, April 1999.

Klein, M, (1996) Risk, Taxpayers, and the Role of Government in Project Finance, World Bank Policy Research Paper No. 1688, December 1996.

Kumar, R. (1998) Debt Sustainability Issues: New Challenges for Liberalising Economies in External Debt Management, Reserve Bank of India, Mumbai.

Lewis, C. and Mody A. (1998) Contingent Liabilities for Infrastructure Projects: Implementing a Risk Management Framework for Government, World Bank, Aug 1998.

Marcus, A. J. and Shaked, I. (1984), The Valuation of FDIC Deposit Insurance Using Option Pricing Estimates, Journal of Money, Credit and Banking.

Merton, R. C. (1990) An Analytic Derivation of the Cost of Deposit Insurance and Loan Guarantees: Application of Modern Option Pricing Theory, Time Finance.

Mody, A. and Patro, D. (1995) Methods of Loan Guarantee Valuation and Accounting, World Bank Discussion Paper No. 116, November 1995.

Mody, A. (2000) Contingent Liabilities in Infrastructure: Lessons of the East Asian Crisis, World Bank, Washington.

Moss, D. A. (1998) Public Risk Management and the Private Sector: An Exploratory Essay, Harvard Business School, Division of Research Working Paper: 98-073 February 1998.

Moss, D. A. (1996) Governments, Markets and Uncertainty: An Historical Approach to Public Risk Management in the United States, Harvard Business School Division of Research Working Paper 97-025, October 1996.

New Zealand Government, Financial Statements (various years), Wellington.

Polackova, H., Ghanem, H., Islam, R. (1999) Fiscal Adjustment and Contingent Government Liabilities – Case Studies of the Czech Republic and Macedonia, World Bank Policy Research Working Paper, 2177 Sept 1999.

Polackova, H. (1999) Contingent Government Liabilities: A Hidden Fiscal Risk, Finance and Development, March 1999, Vol 36, No 1.

Ronn, E. I. and Venna, A. K. (1986), Pricing Risk-Adjusted Deposit Insurance: An Option-Based Model, Journal of Finance 41.

Rowley, K. (1997) Project Pitfalls: Asia's Infrastructure Programmes Would Turn Nasty. Financial Times, 9 December, 1997.

Schick, A. (1999) Budgeting for Fiscal Risk, World Bank Internal Draft, September 1999.

Sebastian, Edwards (1984) LDC Foreign Borrowing and Default Risk: An Empirical Investigation, 1976-80, The American Economic Review, Vol. 74(4), September 1984.

Standard and Poor (1999) Infrastructure Debt After the Crisis, October 1999.

Tanzania: Songo Songo Gas to Electricity Project, World Bank Public Information Document (3TANPA, 125), Dec 1996, Washington.

Thohani, M. (1999) Private Infrastructure, Public Risk, Finance and Development, March 1999, Vol 36, No 1.

Towe, C.M. (1991) The Budgetary Control and Fiscal Impact of Government Contingent Liabilities, IMF Staff Papers Vol. 38 (1).

UK Finance Act, 1998.

UK H. M. Treasury, Fiscal Policy: Public Finances and The Cycle, 1997.

World Bank, Dealing with Public Risk in Private Infrastructure. Edited by Irwin,T., Klein, M., Perry, G. E. and Thobani, M., Washington DC.